MW00329642

WORDS OF STRENGTH AND PROMISE

TO:

FROM:

ON:

WORDS OF STRENGTH AND PROMISE

✝

Amy Bird
Jessica Bordeleau
George Borghardt
Heath Curtis
Christopher Esget
Keith Haney
Hannah Hansen

Molly Lackey
Brandon Metcalf
Matthew Richard
Heather Ruesch
Dave Rueter
Julianna Shults
A. Trevor Sutton

CONCORDIA PUBLISHING HOUSE · SAINT LOUIS

Library of Congress Cataloging-in-Publication Data

Title: Words of strength and promise.

Description: Saint Louis : Concordia Publishing House, [2021] | Summary: "Teens have questions that are specific to their age and stage of life, and they may not feel comfortable asking them of their parents, teachers, pastors, or even friends. The devotions in this book respond to such questions by speaking to the student where he or she is in the moment and by reassuring the reader that he or she is loved by God and forgiven by Jesus and that everyone has similar questions"-- Provided by publisher.

Identifiers: LCCN 2020050524 (print) | LCCN 2020050525 (ebook) | ISBN 9780758667687 (paperback) | ISBN 9780758667694 (ebook)

Subjects: LCSH: Christian teenagers--Religious life--Miscellanea.

Classification: LCC BV4531.3 .W67 2021 (print) | LCC BV4531.3 (ebook) | DDC 248.8/3--dc23

LC record available at https://lccn.loc.gov/2020050524

LC ebook record available at https://lccn.loc.gov/2020050525

2   3   4   5   6   7   8   9   10   11   31   30   29   28   27   26   25   24   23   22

Contents

INTRODUCTION

*As you received Christ Jesus the Lord, so
walk in Him, rooted and built up in Him and
established in the faith, just as you were taught,
abounding in thanksgiving.* (COLOSSIANS 2:6–7)

Here you are, at a time in your life when you're supposed
to *know* things like how to get along, how to make
choices, and what to do in sticky situations. Most of
the time, you *do* know what to think and what to do. After
all, you're not a kid. You're well on your way to being an
autonomous, responsible, independent member of society.

But you have questions. Maybe something happened that
you didn't expect. Perhaps the world suddenly got crazy and you
don't know what to think about it. Or you "knew that" but forgot,
and now you have to deal with some fallout after messing up.

You might be able to go to a trusted adult for answers, and
that person might be able to talk things over with you until all
your questions are answered. And that's good.

However, there may be issues or circumstances that prevent these conversations or make them way too awkward or embarrassing to pursue. That's where this book comes in.

> See to it that no one takes you captive by philosophy and empty deceit, according to human tradition, according to the elemental spirits of the world, and not according to Christ. (Colossians 2:8)

The book you're holding is the result of hours of conversations with people your age and at your stage in life. We talked about difficult, awkward, and embarrassing topics. Seriously, we sat around a table and discussed things we wish we'd known when we were in high school and things that surprised us when we started college or work or service. Nothing was off the table. Those conversations involved every topic we could think of. We asked "what if" and "what about" questions, even if we were embarrassed to verbalize them. And then we reached out to people who would write about these topics with honesty, integrity, dignity, and faith in Christ Jesus.

> Let the peace of Christ rule in your hearts, to which indeed you were called in one body. And be thankful. Let the word of Christ dwell in you richly, teaching and admonishing one another in all wisdom, singing psalms and hymns and spiritual songs, with thankfulness in your hearts to God. And whatever you do, in word or deed, do everything in the name of the Lord

Jesus, giving thanks to God the Father through Him. (Colossians 3:15–17)

So here are fourteen different authors whose hard-won experiences and heartfelt perspectives can guide you through the labyrinth of life. Our prayer is that this book gives you words of strength for your life and assures you of Jesus' promises of forgiveness, mercy, and salvation.

For I know the plans I have for you,

declares the LORD, plans for wel-

fare and not for evil, to give you a

future and a hope. Then you will

call upon Me and come and pray

to Me, and I will hear you.

(JEREMIAH 29:11–12)

IT'S MY MONEY!

Read Romans 11:33–36

How dare he tell *me* what to do with *my* money!" Those words, spoken by an upset church member about his pastor's sermon, could easily be spoken by almost any of us when it comes to the Bible and money. We tend to think that our money is our own and that apart from maybe asking for some of it for the congregation (10 percent max, though), it shouldn't really be talked about during the church service. But these words reveal exactly why believers need to hear about money: we think it's ours.

I'm reminded of the time my son figured out how the library works. Ever since he was born, we have regularly gotten him books from the library. All he knew is that he had a lot of books to read. What he didn't realize was that most of those books went back to the library and were replaced with different ones. He was perfectly happy with the situation until I told him we were going to the library, and I put his books into the library bag. He ran to the bag, pulled out one of his favorites, and yelled, "No! This is mine!" I explained that we just borrow the books from the library, that we don't actually own them. That didn't really get through because the next time I told him we were going to the library, he grabbed books, toys, and anything else he could get his hands on so I wouldn't take them, even though most of those things didn't even belong to the library.

How often do we act like my young son when it comes to money and possessions? We try desperately to hold on to all of it so tightly, thinking it is ours to keep. We want to ignore the rules of the Owner and try to do whatever we want with what we think is ours. Paul reminds us in our text that we are not the owners—God is. "For from Him and through Him and to Him are all things. To Him be glory forever. Amen" (Romans 11:36). Let's note here what Paul does not say—from Him, through Him, and to Him are "*some* things" or "10 percent of my possessions." He also doesn't say "only those things I want to give up" or "those things that are left over after I do what I want." No, what Paul says is "all things." God is the Owner of all things! We are not. This is good news because God is a much better owner than we are. When we live like we're the owners, we become addicted to devices and technology or to having the best car or house; we become so focused on making, spending, and protecting our money that it consumes us. The things we think we own often end up owning us.

God is the Owner of all things, and that means He gets to set the rules. We find those rules laid out in Scripture in places such as the Ten Commandments. We don't get to choose which we think are relevant or which we should follow—we're not the Owner. We don't get to set the rules. God does. This all sounds legalistic, but we know that God is good and gracious. We see that most clearly at Calvary's cross, where God sent His only Son to free us from our sinful desires to use our stuff for our own benefit.

Living as free and forgiven people means we can find the joy in God's ownership, His rules, and His plan. Instead of saying, "How dare he tell me what to do with my money," we can faithfully proclaim, "It's all Yours, Lord! What do You want me to do with it?" Money, possessions, relationships, and all the other gifts God gives us are all reasons we can be thankful to God. They are all gifts He gives us to use well. This means wisely using all that we are and all that we have to love and serve those around us, that they would know Christ and His love for them.

Lord, it's all Yours! Help us to be faithful with all Your blessings!

IN THE GRIP

God shows His love for us in that while we were
still sinners, Christ died for us. (ROMANS 5:8)

I n Romans, Paul recounts his struggles with sin. The apostle, saint, and great evangelist is open and honest: "For I do not understand my own actions. For I do not do what I want, but I do the very thing I hate" (7:15). This very well could be a motif of the addict—especially the Christian addict.

Whether this realization returns the morning after yet another night of binge drinking or just following the loss of another paycheck blown getting high, it is not easy to understand ourselves. How is it that we always forget our regret? Why do we keep going back to the same place of pain and loss?

Now you might think that this topic is not relevant to you, and perhaps you are right, but before moving on, consider this: Have you ever pulled out your phone and then wondered why? Is there a game that keeps drawing you back, perhaps a social media app you just can't go a day or even an hour without?

The human race is creative when it comes to inventing new addictions and ways to deliver them. If you have ever regretted time or money you put into something meaningless and find yourself regretting it time and time again, you may have found your addiction.

> Wretched man that I am! Who will deliver me from this body of death? (Romans 7:24)

Answering his own question, Paul continues in Romans 8:1–4:

> There is therefore now no condemnation for those who are in Christ Jesus. For the law of the Spirit of life has set you free in Christ Jesus from the law of sin and death. For God has done what the law, weakened by the flesh, could not do. By sending His own Son in the likeness of sinful flesh and for sin, He condemned sin in the flesh, in order that the righteous requirement of the law might be fulfilled in us, who walk not according to the flesh but according to the Spirit.

In Christ, we are no longer bound by addiction. Don't think that sounds easy—this does not mean that addiction immediately goes away. The physiological and biochemical realities remain. Just as Paul still struggled in his sin, we still face daily temptation, but we are not in bondage to that sin.

The whispered lies of the evil one remind us what we have done, but they cannot hold us captive. In Christ, we have full forgiveness. We are declared righteous, though we have yet to demonstrate any righteousness of our own. As Paul states in

Romans 5:8, "God shows His love for us in that while we were still sinners, Christ died for us."

Amid addiction of all kinds, God comes in Christ to claim us for His own, freeing us to seek support and helping us to break from the ongoing temptation of sin. "For you did not receive the spirit of slavery to fall back into fear, but you have received the Spirit of adoption as sons, by whom we cry, 'Abba! Father!'" (Romans 8:15).

WHERE OUR ANGER FINDS ITS END

I t has been said that anger is a secondary emotion. That is to say, anger is typically a strong feeling that comes as a result of something else, such as injustice, lack of control, feeling threatened, or being disrespected. When something is not the way we think it should be, we might feel angry.

It is important to remember that anger is not sin, and it is an appropriate response to many situations and circumstances of life. Take Jesus, for example. He got angry but did so without sin. He got angry about the corruption in the temple. He was angry with the false teaching of the religious leaders. And He was especially angry at the death of Lazarus.

In the Gospel of John, chapter 11, Jesus came to the tomb of His friend Lazarus. Jesus was deeply moved, and verse 35 tells us that He cried. In the original language, the text says Jesus not only wept about the death of Lazarus, but He also "snorted" at death with disgust. Indeed, He grunted, was disgusted, and was angry with death. He expressed anger toward the tomb of Lazarus because death was not the way it should have been for Lazarus. God did not create humanity for death.

What this means is that we can take comfort when we, too, are angry at death and the effects of sin and death in our lives.

We are not alone, for Jesus was angered over the great enemy that death is because it is not the plan God has for humanity.

And so, when we experience anger and shake our fist at death and cry out in pain, we can remember that we have a Savior who is also angry at death. When we punch at death or weep over death, we have a Savior who understands. When we clench our jaw or want to collapse inward on ourselves, Christ knows, for He angered and wept as well.

It brings us comfort to know that the Lord Jesus Christ understands. To express our anger and vocalize our sorrow is healthy and good. However, we must keep in mind that after we have gritted our teeth, cursed at death, and shaken our fists—death is still there, grinning at us as the victor. We cry; death smirks. We snarl; death laughs. Our anger only responds and cannot overcome or tame the mighty enemy that is death. It is a small noise of disapproval against a giant, undefeatable cacophony.

Jesus, though, is not limited to the emotion of anger as you and I are. Instead, He angered at death to the point that He did something about it.

There, amid the grieving crowd at the place where Lazarus had been buried for four days, God the Son stepped forward and spoke toward the dark tomb, "Lazarus, come out" (v. 43). And so Lazarus did. For every time the Lord speaks, His words do what they say.

This is possible for Jesus Christ because His frustration over death and His love for you moved Him to the jaws of death and the sting of sin. Otherwise stated, His anger over humanity's predicament of sin and love for humanity led Him to the lair of death and a collision with sin. There at the cross on Mount Calvary, the Son of God was not some sort of sissy Savior; He was not a victim we should feel sorry for. Instead, He did what we could not do; He confronted sin and death on our behalf. The Giver of life warred with the enemy that is death on our behalf—and He defeated it. Death became an obedient servant to the Word Incarnate.

And so, take comfort, baptized saints! Your anger has its end in Christ, who did something to remedy sin and death. He bled, died, and rose on your behalf to be the victor over your sin, to take away the sting of death.

So, let us not sin in our anger; rather, let us echo this cry: "O death, where is your victory?" (1 Corinthians 15:55) while remembering that the Conqueror of death even angers on our behalf.

ANGER WARPS THE IMAGE OF GOD

The Fifth Commandment is unmistakable: You shall not murder. The challenge among the scribes and Pharisees is that they interpreted this command in its narrowest sense. The only way to break it was through the shedding of innocent blood. As long as they didn't cross that line, they were safe. But Jesus says the commandment extends to "emotional murder":

> You have heard that it was said to those of old, "You shall not murder; and whoever murders will be liable to judgment." But I say to you that everyone who is angry with his brother will be liable to judgment; whoever insults his brother will be liable to the council; and whoever says, "You fool!" will be liable to the hell of fire. (Matthew 5:21–22)

Now that is a game changer. If resentment and anger against someone are included in the definition of murder, none of us is innocent.

Anger is one of the most powerful emotions, and as Jesus points out in Matthew, unchecked anger has repercussions.

For example, one act of outrage that started as a spark on a baseball field inflamed the crowd in the stands and burned down a stadium.

Tommy Tucker, a mouthy first baseman for the Baltimore Orioles, was well known for dirty play. On May 15, 1894, in the third inning against the Boston Beaneaters, Tucker rounded second and slid hard into third baseman John McGraw. Equally aggressive, McGraw responded with a kick to Tucker's face as he made the tag. The benches emptied as both teams joined the fray. Fans jumped to their feet to watch. And with all eyes on third base, no one noticed that some boys had accidentally started a fire under the right-field stands. By the time the fire was noticed, it was too late. Most of the ballpark and two hundred other buildings were damaged in what became known as the Great Roxbury Fire.

Anger is an offense that perverts the likeness of God, which we were created to reflect. The emotion that best reflects the nature of God is *shalom*, peace.

Shalom is better translated into English as "flourishing." Shalom happens when all the conditions of God's creation are such that everything He made functions and thrives exactly as He formed and created it to do. You recognize this during those moments when it appears as though everything around you in life is tuned exactly as God intends it to be—everything thrives and grows and flourishes. That's *shalom*. This is what we pray God will restore to His creation. This is what those who gather in the presence of God are looking for. The reflection of our worship directed to our triune God is best fulfilled by His response of shalom-flourishing. That is the picture we encounter in Isaiah 32:16–17:

Then justice will dwell in the wilderness, and righteousness abide in the fruitful field. And the effect of righteousness will be peace, and the result of righteousness, quietness and trust forever.

Heavenly Father, Your peace passes all my understanding. When anger rises within me, please calm my mind and soften my heart with Your tender words. Fill my whole life with Your perfect peace. May Your peace rather than my frustration shape my emotions. With Your Holy Spirit in my life, I can overcome anger. May I reveal Your nature, being slow to anger and rich in steadfast love. Look upon me and cause Your face to shine upon me. Through Jesus Christ, our Lord. Amen.

"DON'T BE ANXIOUS" DOESN'T HELP

I am weary with my moaning;
every night I flood my bed with tears;
I drench my couch with my weeping.
My eye wastes away because of grief;
it grows weak because of all my foes.
Depart from me, all you workers of evil,
for the LORD has heard the
sound of my weeping.
The LORD has heard my plea;
the LORD accepts my prayer.

(PSALM 6:6–9)

Recently, I went through a really difficult season of life. I moved away from all my friends and family, was stuck in a horrible job, and had to build a new life from the ground up (it's hard out here for an introvert).

During the first six months of that transition, I was tired, moody, sad, anxious, irritable, and overwhelmed. Those feelings lasted for a long time—long enough that people in my life grew concerned for me and encouraged me to seek help.

I went to the doctor, and she diagnosed me with depression and anxiety, prescribed medication, and recommended that I see a counselor.

It's been six months since then (longer than that by the time you'll read this), and I am feeling more emotionally stable, so I'm able to work with my therapist through some hang-ups.

If you've ever struggled with any aspect of your mental health, I empathize with you. I know how hard it can be to pull yourself out of bed and get dressed. To drive your car. To think thoughts that are scary and unwanted.

Those things were certainly hard for me during that low season. But do you know what one of the hardest parts of my mental health journey was? A lot of people tried to slap a Bible verse on top of my anxiety like a Band-Aid. They'd quote verses such as "do not be anxious about anything" (Philippians 4:6) or "do not be anxious about your life" (Matthew 6:25) and somehow expect that to make me less anxious.

Do you know what *doesn't* make anxiety go away? Telling someone to not be anxious (even if it is a Bible verse).

But do you know what *does* help someone manage anxiety or depression? Medication. Therapy. Prayers.

It's important to know when to seek medical help for your mental health. There is absolutely no shame in taking care of your mind like you take care of your body. There is most definitely a place for medical care. But there's also a need for spiritual care. We just have to make sure to do it the right way.

I was most encouraged not when friends tried to fix my mental health or comfort me with a cherry-picked Bible verse, but rather when they just said, "That stinks. I'm praying for you. Let me know how I can help you best."

Prayer is powerful because we have a powerful God who hears our prayers. And knowing that I have friends and family who were faithfully praying for me during that time when I couldn't pray for myself was such a comfort to me.

I related a lot to the psalmist in the verses for this devotion, and maybe you have too:

"Every night I flood my bed with tears"—yup. Been there, done that.

"I drench my couch with my weeping"—same.

So many people think that being a Christian means always being happy and perfect and having your life together and not being anxious about anything. But you are still a child of God, even when you're struggling. Even when you can't pray for yourself because you're so overwhelmed. Sometimes, our tears can be our prayers. From our psalm: "For the LORD has heard the sound of my weeping. The LORD has heard my plea."

God gives us His Word, pastors, and the community of believers. But He also gives us doctors, counselors, therapists, and medicine. My prayer is that as you navigate your own mental health, you're able to be healed in mind and soul. Even if your prayer is just tears and no words, pray to God as often as you can. God *will* hear your weeping, and He'll comfort you.

A WHOLE NEW WORLD

And I heard a loud voice from the throne saying,
"Behold, the dwelling place of God is with man.
He will dwell with them, and they will be His people,
and God Himself will be with them as their God.
He will wipe away every tear from their eyes, and
death shall be no more, neither shall there
be mourning, nor crying, nor pain anymore,
for the former things have passed away."

And He who was seated on the throne said, "Behold,
I am making all things new." (REVELATION 21:3–5)

A lot of bad stuff is happening in the world right now. I'm not sure exactly when you're reading this, but I can guess that something big is happening.

From natural disasters to wars to diseases to school shootings—it's all a little too much to handle.

We live in a stressful time. There's no denying that. Bad things happen every day, and we hear about all of these events nearly instantly. It's impossible to filter our feeds enough never to see an upsetting news story.

These events affect us so deeply and personally, even if we don't realize it. We might feel overwhelmed at times, as if God isn't present in the world. We might catch ourselves wondering *If God is so good, why do all these bad things keep happening? How could an all-powerful God let children starve and people die in earthquakes and cities be destroyed by wildfires and pandemics kill a million people?*

Reread the verses at the beginning of this devotion. These verses come from the Book of Revelation, and these specific sentences describe what the new heaven and the new earth will look like. The new heaven and the new earth are different than the typical heaven we think of (angels in the clouds with harps)—it's actually what the earth we live on will be like after Jesus comes back.

We'll be on this earth, with Jesus, except it will be completely different. Those verses say there will be no tears or death, no crying or pain! It's pretty hard to imagine a world like that now, amid all the terrible things that are going on.

One of the promises that is made over and over again in the Bible is that Jesus will come back. And when He does, we'll get to live with Him forever in peace and harmony and joy! And after looking at these promises in Revelation, I, for one, would like to be on that earth. I'd like to be on that earth *now*!

Although we won't get to experience that great new heaven and new earth until Jesus returns, know that God is dwelling among us in the world still. Our King Jesus is reigning and ruling over this world as we speak. It is so filled with sin and darkness that sometimes it's hard to see Him.

But every time you gather for church or Bible study or youth group, God is dwelling among you! When you volunteer at a food pantry or rake leaves in someone's yard, you're being Jesus' hands and feet in this world. When you pray, God is inviting you into conversation with Him.

Bad things will continue to happen as long as we live on this sinful earth. There will still be viruses and hurricanes and death. But we can look forward to the day Jesus comes back and restores everything and makes all things new! In the meantime, know that God is still present, and He's dwelling among you right now amid our messy world.

LET THE WORD WORK

For I delivered to you as of first importance what I also received: that Christ died for our sins in accordance with the Scriptures, that He was buried, that He was raised on the third day in accordance with the Scriptures, and that He appeared to Cephas, then to the twelve. Then He appeared to more than five hundred brothers at one time, most of whom are still alive, though some have fallen asleep. Then He appeared to James, then to all the apostles. Last of all, as to one untimely born, He appeared also to me. (1 CORINTHIANS 15:3–8)

Being a believer in Jesus doesn't mean taking a leap of faith. Believing is not without evidence. Christianity is based on eyewitness testimony of Jesus' death and resurrection (see 1 Corinthians 15:1–8). Being a believer means that, based on His past actions, you believe God's promises. You deem Him trustworthy.

It's like if your mom promises to pick you up from soccer practice. You believe her and are totally confident she will be there, even though it's something that will take place in the future. Why do you believe her? Because she's done it before, and you have her word that she will be there. That's no blind leap; it's confidence in her character.

Our friends who aren't believers don't need to "just have faith." They need to know the testimony of the eyewitnesses of the resurrection and learn the character of the One to whom the Scriptures testify.

Don't stand in judgment of the nonbeliever or someone who believes something erroneous. Remember what you learned about preparing to receive the Lord's Supper: you have to examine yourself. When dealing with non-Christians, remember that every Divine Service begins by confessing your own sins. Or as Paul says, "If we judged ourselves truly, we would not be judged" (1 Corinthians 11:31). Don't judge others. Judge yourself, and remember that you are a sinner.

When you have opportunity, explain the Commandments of God as a humble person who is guilty of breaking them. You can explain why God has given them: His intention is to love and protect us with His Word. God's Commandments are like when your mom told you not to play in the street. She gave you a command because she didn't want to see you get hurt. We can see that our friends who are breaking, for example, the Sixth Commandment feel like they're having fun, but they are ultimately damaging themselves for meaningful relationships leading to holy marriage.

When people challenge our Christianity, the goal is not to win the argument. The person with whom you dialogue is someone for whom Christ died. Help them see that there is another way of looking at the argument they are posing. Be willing to not know an answer. "That's a good point. I haven't thought about that. Could we talk about this again in a few days?" Few people will change their minds all at once.

I always keep in mind a man I visited as a pastor. He had told me he would never believe a key aspect of Christian teaching. "No matter what you say," he told me, "no matter what Bible passage you quote to me, I will never change my mind!" A few years later, he was in the hospital, and I went to visit him. He asked, "Pastor, do you remember when I told you I'd never change my mind?" I told him I remembered. "Well," he said, "I've changed my mind." It was my privilege to give him Communion, and he died a few days later. I didn't change his mind by arguing with him to make a point. Over time, the Holy Spirit changed his mind. The Word works. Let it work. Try to get out of the way of the Word.

Some people just want to argue. In some places, like certain schools, this can leave us feeling marginalized and alone. That hurts, but it shouldn't surprise us. "Indeed, all who desire to live a godly life in Christ Jesus will be persecuted, while evil people and impostors will go on from bad to worse, deceiving and being deceived" (2 Timothy 3:12–13). When Jesus taught people about Him being the bread of life, many of His disciples left Him (see John 6:35–69).

When you feel alone, stay grounded by going to church, joining a Bible study at your school, or calling your pastor. When you get into college, you might be uncomfortable talking about these problems with older people; perhaps they seem out of touch. They may not understand exactly what you're going through, but they've faced similar things in their own lives. Lean on their wisdom and experience. And ask them to pray for you! They will be delighted to do so.

The LORD is my strength and my song, and He has become my salvation; this is my God, and I will praise Him, my father's God, and I will exalt Him.

(EXODUS 15:2)

WHY AREN'T YOU JUST CATHOLIC?

You're talking with a classmate or co-worker—or maybe you've even invited a friend to attend the Divine Service with you—and then they pop that awkward question: "Why aren't you just Catholic?"

Of course, they mean "big C" Catholic or the Roman Catholic Church. You are a part of the church catholic, the universal Church, after all. To be fair, you can't really even be upset at them for asking. Maybe it's because we share a lot of the same "smells and bells"—a lot of our hymns are old; our pastors wear the same kinds of shirts and vestments; we use the same funny Latin words like *Introit* and *Agnus Dei*; we have the same things in the church building, such as altars and chalices; and we celebrate sacraments such as Confession and Absolution. Maybe your friend is Catholic, so it all seems similar; maybe your friend is Baptist, so it all seems different; or maybe your friend is an atheist, so it all seems the same.

Why aren't you just Catholic? Well, there's an easy answer you can give: in 1517, an unassuming Augustinian friar and theology professor in Wittenberg, Germany, named Martin Luther wrote the Ninety-Five Theses—a list of ninety-five things that burdened his conscience about the practice of indulgences.

Rather than buying remission of the temporal punishment of sin (i.e., purgatory), Luther believed that the Christian's whole life should be one of repentance. Fast-forward: this same monk is now excommunicated, married to a nun, and starting a church based on Scripture alone, faith alone, and grace alone.

But that's the easy answer. Rather, it's the answer to the easy question. Instead, the question isn't why aren't you just Catholic, but why are you Lutheran? Why are you, personally, Lutheran?

Thankfully, you know how to answer. You're not Roman Catholic—or any other denomination, for that matter—but instead are Lutheran because you, like the people who wrote the Augsburg Confession some five hundred years ago, believe that

> people cannot be justified before God by their own strength, merits, or works. People are freely justified for Christ's sake, through faith, when they believe that they are received into favor and that their sins are forgiven for Christ's sake. By His death, Christ made satisfaction for our sins. God counts this faith for righteousness in His sight. (AC IV 1–3)

And that's a big deal.

> Upon this article everything that we teach and practice depends, in opposition to the pope, the devil, and the whole world. Therefore, we must be certain and not doubt this doctrine. Otherwise, all is lost, and the pope, the devil, and all adversaries win the victory and the right over us. (SA II I 5)

And what does all that mean? Jesus, God in human flesh, was born, lived, and ministered—perfectly and sinlessly—all for you. And then He *died*. Why? In order to make "satisfaction for [y]our sins," or to pay the price, face the consequences, die your death—for you. Why? Not because you did anything. Not because you do good works. Not because you accepted Him into your heart or gave Him your life or anything like that. Instead, it was out of abundant love. Nothing about you, everything about Jesus! Romans 5:8 says, "but God shows His love for us in that while we were still sinners, Christ died for us."

And that's what it's all about. If you get that wrong, you get everything wrong. That's why you're not Roman Catholic—because the Roman Catholic Church still, sadly, teaches that your works contribute to your salvation. And that's why you're Lutheran—because you know that it's all about Jesus. Any church, denomination, or teacher that tells you it's about anything except Jesus *alone* is wrong. If it's Jesus plus you, whether that's your works, your will, or your heart, that's not Jesus *alone*. It's got to be justification by faith *alone* in Christ *alone* through grace *alone*, or it's nothing.

That's what you mean when you say "Justification is the article on which the church stands or falls," that popular Lutheran saying. Justification is all about Jesus, and Jesus is "the founder and perfecter of [y]our faith" (Hebrews 12:2). Being Lutheran means you are always looking to Jesus, not your works, to find your salvation and your comfort. And that's why you're Lutheran.

ALL THE SINGLE LADIES (AND DUDES)

How long, O LORD? Will You forget me forever?
How long will You hide Your face from me?
How long must I take counsel in my soul
and have sorrow in my heart all the day?

(PSALM 13:1–2)

W hen you're single, you hear a lot of clichés that don't really help you feel any better about being single.

· "Don't worry, God will send the right person your way in His timing!"

· "You know, Paul and Jesus were single!"

· "You're still so young—you'll find someone!"

· "But you're so cute and sweet! I'm surprised someone hasn't locked you down yet!"

See what I mean? These meaningless phrases don't really do anything for anyone. They probably annoy you more than anything else. So this devotion isn't going to focus on any of that. Instead, we're going to look at three truths. At first, they might be hard to hear, but please read all the way to the end.

Our first truth is one that perhaps few people have acknowledged in your life: *being single is hard*. It's not hard for everyone, but it's hard for a lot of people. You can feel lonely, unworthy, isolated, and left out. It's not always "thirty, flirty, and thriving"!

Our second truth was hard for me to accept when I first heard it: *God does not promise that you will get married.*

That's a hard reality to face, I know. And that's hard to believe when having a boyfriend or girlfriend seems so appealing, and everyone except you is dating someone. It doesn't exactly help to know that marriage is not a given. In fact, it might make it worse to know there is an option of being single forever.

(I hope you're not too down after reading those last few paragraphs. We still have one last truth.)

Here's our final truth: *your life is just as valuable when you're single.*

God loves you whether or not you're taken, and He's going to use you in this season of singleness, no matter how long it lasts. I know it's hard to see, but God is working in your heart to draw you closer to Him and serve your neighbor, whether you realize it or not.

I close this devotion by saying that you can be sad about being single. Maybe you haven't heard that before because older people are telling you "these are the best years of your life" or "enjoy your freedom while you're young." I know that none of those words help, and I just want to reassure you that it's okay to be sad.

But the next step is the most important: you should take your sadness to God. The first two verses of Psalm 13 are at the beginning of this devotion, but go ahead and read the whole psalm. It's not very long.

At one point or another, you've probably felt like verses 1 and 2. "How long will I be single, God? How long will I have to sit on the sidelines and watch everyone else pair off while I'm stuck here alone?"

Now read verses 5 and 6 again. Notice how the psalmist's "problem" hasn't been solved—he's still experiencing whatever is making him cry out to God. But despite that, he shifts his perspective and begins to praise God in the middle of his agony.

He's trusting. Rejoicing. Even singing! He's remembering the things God has already given him—steadfast love and salvation. In a situation of fear and sadness, he clings to the only things that are a glimmer of hope in a dark time, the things he knows are true.

I hope that in your singleness, amid your struggle, you're able to praise God. That you're able to remember the blessings He has given you, even when you're sad. That you're able to see His hand working in a hard season of life.

LET THE LITTLE (AND BIG) CHILDREN COME TO ME

One of my all-time favorite works of art is Fritz von Uhde's 1885 oil painting *Let the Little Children Come to Me*. Take a moment to look it up. Von Uhde, a nineteenth-century German Lutheran painter, depicted biblical scenes in his contemporary context with a stunning effect. In *Let the Little Children Come to Me*, Christ holds the hand of one little girl while embracing another who buries her head in His lap. A crowd of children and their parents surround Him in a living room. The point of all this? Jesus is present, for you—even among little children, even almost two thousand or so years after He first uttered: "let the little children come to Me" (Matthew 19:14).

And more than a century after this painting was created, more than two millennia after Christ's life, death, resurrection, and ascension, Jesus is still saying "let the little children come to Me."

The teenage and adolescent years are just weird. Are you now an adult or still a child? Are you still treated as though you're not *quite* old enough for some things? And what about when those things are church-related? You've been confirmed and all, but are you *really* old enough to "get" the Gospel? If we tell you the Gospel, you'll just use it as a license for sin, if you even understand that much, right?

Jesus says, "Let the little children come to Me." He might as well say, "Let the big children come to Me too." You might still be a child under the eyes of the law or in the eyes of your parents or relatives or older people you know. But you're also a child in God's eyes—and you will always be a child in God's eyes. What does that mean? Not that you're too immature or not smart enough to understand the Gospel. Instead, it means that it is absolutely imperative that you hear the Gospel. Being a child of God—having the Good News preached to you—looks like the two little girls so near to Jesus in that painting.

The Gospel is the simple Word of God proclaiming you totally free, totally clean, totally guiltless, totally sinless, totally perfect now and in eternity. It means that, even though you were conceived in sin, even though you are sinful and unclean in your innermost being, even though you have committed and continue to commit evil all the days of your (so-far short) life, Jesus took all of it away onto Himself, taking your punishment—death!—and dying for you on the cross. He then returned from the dead on the third day so that there would be no more death for you. Sure, you will fall asleep one day, but on the Last Day, Christ Jesus will raise you. And don't forget that Jesus ascended into heaven, which is a two-for-one great gift. Fully glorified after subjecting himself to humiliation on our behalf, Christ now reigns as supreme King of this world, Lord over all, so that He, in His Word and Sacraments, can be truly present in our lives. This is true whether it's in the waters of Baptism through His Word, in the sound waves of that spoken Absolution bouncing around on your eardrum, or in the

Lord's Supper with His very body and blood. Not only that, but Jesus' reign in heaven is where your soul will go when you die: to rest in His tender arms until the Last Day, when you will be raised to live in eternal perfection and blessedness with Christ and with the redeemed.

The Formula of Concord defines the Gospel this way:

> The Gospel is properly the kind of teaching that shows what a person who has not kept the Law (and therefore is condemned by it) is to believe. It teaches that Christ has paid for and made satisfaction for all sins [Romans 5:9]. Christ has gained and acquired for an individual—without any of his own merit—forgiveness of sins, righteousness that avails before God, and eternal life [Romans 5:10]. (FC Ep V 4)

This is yours as a child of God, no matter if you're an infant or a "big kid" or an adult or somewhere in between. Cling to it. Cherish it. And let no one take it away from you.

OUR SUFFERINGS ARE ONLY A LITTLE WHILE

I have said these things to you, that in
Me you may have peace. In the world you
will have tribulation. But take heart;
I have overcome the world. (JOHN 16:33)

In the Gospel of John, Jesus talks about the cross of all believers. The word *cross* refers to the suffering and pain we experience because we are Christians. These crosses are things such as persecution, pressure, slander, accusations, attacks, and so forth.

It's no secret that the life of a Christian in this world is not a long, pleasant walk on the beach. The world hated Jesus, and so it will hate you.

You may be tempted to try to avoid bearing the cross that the world and the devil lay on the backs of Christians. There are many ways Christians try to do this. For example, when the cross of suffering comes, you may be tempted to grow impatient or frustrated and even leave the Christian Church. What if you do not leave the Church but stay faithful instead? Is there any comfort?

Yes, there is comfort! Jesus says clearly in John 16 that all of this life under the sun—with its crosses—will last for only "a little while." Jesus does not call us to flee or fight these hardships. Neither does He call us to water things down to avoid suffering. And Jesus does not say that the crosses will always be removed in this life. Instead, He says that this life will not endure. You and I cannot escape the torments of the devil and the sinful world this side of heaven; however, they do have an end, and their end is in "a little while."

You see, there will be a time when you will no longer remember the anguishes of this life under the sun. Your sorrow will not last forever; instead, it will be turned to eternal joy. You may find yourself in darkness now, but take comfort that there will be a dawn of glory. Christ has come to be the Savior, and He understands our sufferings more than anyone else.

As we continue to walk through this life under the sun, cling to the promises of God's Word—the promises that are for you as a beloved child of God. Step forward to receive the Sacrament of the Altar—it is given and shed for you. Remember your Baptism—where God's name was placed upon you. Patiently endure any misfortune, comforting yourself with the truth that the Lord is with you in His Word and Sacraments. He promises never to leave you or forsake you.

Comfort yourself with Jesus' word that this life is only "a little while." You are living in the little while of this life. Know that as tough as life gets, the Lord holds not only the beginning but also the end of this world. He is the beginning and the end; therefore, we need not fear what is in the middle because it lasts only a little while. Nothing in all of creation can separate you from the love of God in Christ Jesus.

IF ONLY . . .

*Not that I am speaking of being in need, for
I have learned in whatever situation I am
to be content. I know how to be brought
low, and I know how to abound. In any and
every circumstance, I have learned the secret
of facing plenty and hunger, abundance
and need. I can do all things through Him
who strengthens me.* (PHILIPPIANS 4:11–13)

If only I could make the team, then I'd have friends." "If only he would ask me out, then I'd feel good about myself." "If only I could get the latest phone, then they wouldn't make fun of me." If only . . . if only . . .

What "if only" situation are you currently in? We can easily devise a plan for how to make life better *if only* we could change one thing. *If only* this one wish would come true, then our troubles would go away.

Have you ever had your "if only" desire fulfilled? What happened next? Was that the end to your "if only" dreaming?

Not for me. When one of my wishes was fulfilled, I discovered that my "if only" plan was just one step in a list of ongoing "if onlys." Once that guy asked me out, I developed a new set of insecurities that I needed validated. Dating a cute boy didn't solve my underlying concerns.

Letting myself continue down the path of "if only" thinking led to more "if only" thinking. It never came to an end. Rather, I discovered more discontent and still coveted what God hadn't given me.

Seeking to better our situation can be admirable and a way we steward—or manage—the gifts God gives us. However, "if only" thinking can also be dangerous when it leads us to lusting after what we don't have at the cost of disregarding the blessings we do have.

We read in 2 Samuel 11 how this played out for King David. David was a successful ruler and king over all of Israel. Whatever he wanted, he got. Then, one late afternoon as he stood on his rooftop and looked out over his kingdom, he noticed a beautiful woman bathing. David already had several wives but, upon seeing Bathsheba, immediately wanted her as well. While it's not recorded for us in Scripture, it's easy to imagine David's "if only" thinking. "If only I had Bathsheba as my wife, I'd be happy." Or, "If only I could have this most beautiful woman, it would prove I'm the most important man."

But Bathsheba was Uriah's wife. For David to get what he wanted, he had to lie, deceive, and eventually have Uriah killed. "If only" thinking led David down the slippery slope of sin and unfaithfulness to God. He became immoral, unethical, and criminal.

The apostle Paul describes another way of thinking in his Letter to the Church in Philippi. Paul says he's learned the secret to contentment in every situation—whether he had it all or had nothing to show for it. Paul learned that regardless of what God gives or doesn't give, contentment is possible when we "rejoice in the Lord always" (Philippians 4:4). Paul isn't suggesting we pretend everything is okay when it's not. Rather, he says, "in everything by prayer and supplication with thanksgiving let your requests be made known to God" (v. 6). Cultivating a mentality that looks for reasons to be thankful even in the worst of situations changes the way we view all of our circumstances so we recognize the blessings God *has* given us. In return, Paul says God's peace will guard our hearts and minds (v. 7).

We can exchange worry for peace and "if only" thinking for contentment in Christ.

As you remain connected to Christ through prayer and the receiving of the Word and Sacrament, ask the Spirit to cultivate in you a spirit of contentment—a way of answering "if only" thinking with a thankful "nevertheless." It might look like this:

*If only I could make the team, then I'd have friends—*nevertheless, Jesus is a friend who is closer than any brother. Thanks, Jesus!

*If only he would ask me out, then I'd feel good about myself—*nevertheless, God loves me more perfectly than any person ever could. Thank You, Father!

*If only I could get the latest phone, then they wouldn't make fun of me—*nevertheless, God says I'm wonderfully made and has welcomed me into His family. Thanks, Holy Spirit, for clothing me in Christ's righteousness, something far greater than any passing fad.

Let's end this devotion with a short activity. Name ten things you're thankful for, and then turn each one into a prayer of thanksgiving to God. Thanks for all You give us, God!

MEMENTO MORI

Maybe you're lucky. Maybe you don't know much about death. Death sure was on the news a lot in 2020, as the world faced the COVID-19 (or coronavirus) pandemic. It was certainly scary and horrible—in large part because we don't normally have to deal with death on such a large scale. But even in times without the looming specter of a mass plague, death lurks, often unnoticed, in the shadows of our lives. According to the CDC, somewhere around 1,770 people die every day in the United States from heart disease. Another 1,640 or so die every day from cancer. About 465 die from an unintentional accident, such as a car crash or a fall. Every day in the US, 129 people kill themselves. Suicide is now the tenth leading cause of death in America.[1] And did you know that somewhere between a third to a half of all fertilized zygotes—so, a baby, whether that baby is one cell in size or thirty-nine weeks old—die of natural causes in utero? And that's not counting abortions. The Planned Parenthood Federation of America performed 345,672 abortions—killed 345,672 babies—in the 2018 fiscal

---

[1]   Melonie Heron, "Deaths: Leading Causes for 2017," National Vital Statistics Reports, vol. 68, num. 6, cdc.gov/nchs/data/nvsr/nvsr68/nvsr68_06-508.pdf

year, around 947 every single day.[2] And that's not counting the unknown number of babies killed by abortifacient drugs. Maybe this is news to you.

There is an ancient Latin phrase, *memento mori*. It literally means "remember death," but it is usually translated "remember you will die." It's so easy to forget. We are surrounded by, even swimming in, death. It begins to look normal to us. We speak in ways that hide the reality of death: have you ever noticed how people "pass away" or "pass on"; they almost never *die*? And not just the sick or the elderly die; young people, healthy people, *all* people are living life balanced on the head of a pin, in the delicate dance of our fragile mortality. *Memento mori*—remember you will die.

What does it mean *to die* anyway? We don't know a whole lot about death, other than that it is the separation of the soul from the body, a state that God never intended. Romans 6:23 tells us that "the wages of sin is death." As to the experience of death itself, we don't know much about the actual experience of death, but we know a lot more about the effects it has. A dead person can't talk to his loved ones anymore, can't protect them or be protected, can't read or write or dance, or mindlessly scroll Facebook or stream movies or laugh or kiss or smile. It is the ultimate loss of control, control over the self, over others, over the world, over God. We are utterly creatures—created, not creators—in death.

Memento mori—remember you will die. But while we're learning Latin phrases, let's learn another: *memento mortuus est*, Latin for "remember He has died." Jesus Christ, the Divine Logos,

---

2   Planned Parenthood, Annual Report 2019-2019, plannedparenthood.org/uploads/filer_public/2e/da/2eda3f50-82aa-4ddb-acce-c2854c4ea80b/2018-2019_annual_report.pdf

the Word of God, very God of very God, became a man, became incarnate or in-the-flesh—in your flesh—for you. Why? To redeem you. Not just your soul or your spirit or your mind, but *all of you*, flesh, blood, cells, mitochondria, arms and legs, smiles and laughs. You are both the incorporeal (not-body) and the corporeal (body) bits of you, and Jesus has saved *all of that*. Saved from what? From sin and from the wages of sin—death. How? By dying, for you. *Memento mortuus est*, remember He has died, nailed to a tree, sinless, deathless God dying sinful man's death.

Death is inevitable (unless, of course, Jesus returns first). Sooner or later, you *will* die. But, as a baptized, precious child of our Lord, you will rest in the arms of Jesus, the same nail-scarred, crucified arms of the God-man, the Christ, who died the death you deserve in exchange for giving you His eternal, perfect life. That is exactly what you have now—and what you'll have in the life to come, when Christ raises you back from the dead, soul meeting body once more, this time to live in everlasting peace and blessedness. *Memento mori*. Remember you will die. *Memento mortuus est*. Remember He has died.

And one more: *memento vivere*—remember you will live.

WHO ARE YOU?

You are Christ's, and Christ is God's. (1 Corinthians 3:23)

You are not heterosexual. You are not gay or bisexual. You are not a guy or a girl. Not because gender is fluid. And not because such things don't matter. They do—a lot. But these words don't ultimately describe who you are.

You may be a man or a woman. You may be a son or daughter. You may be straight or gay. You may be tall or short. Other people describe you these ways, but their adjectives aren't who you are. The world may label you in this way or that way, but the world does not define you.

What you have and have not done doesn't define you either. You aren't successful. You aren't a failure. You aren't fat. You aren't skinny. You aren't stupid, smart, good looking, or ugly—even if you sometimes feel like these things.

"You are Christ's, and Christ is God's." You are baptized. God has put His name on you. He has identified you as His own. You are His. As one of my professors, Dr. Norman Nagel, used to say, "You are who you are because Jesus did what He did for you."

You are defined, you are identifiable, by God's name put on you at your Baptism.

Christ lived His life for you, and He died the death you deserve for your sin. All that God requires of you was done for you by Jesus. All the punishment due to you from God, all that you deserve from God, was taken on by Jesus and died with Him. He rose from the dead on Easter morning, and you rose with Him in the waters of Baptism. You are who you are; you are defined by what Jesus did for you.

All the other things and labels you wrestle with in this life pertaining to your gender must be considered within the context of your Baptism. "You are Christ's, and Christ is God's." Say it. Believe it. Creed it. That's who you are. Another way of thinking of this is simply to say like we do every Sunday, "In the name of the Father and of the Son and of the Holy Spirit." That's to remember whose you are: God's redeemed child.

When you define yourself by what you do and don't do, when you define yourself by your failures or successes or the orientation you feel is truly you—that is when you've already lost. As soon as you define yourself by what you are and what you aren't, apart from Jesus, you provide an opportunity for Satan to pull you out of the safety of the Christian Church.

"You are Christ's, and Christ is God's." That's who you are. Jesus defines you! You wear God's name. You are His own child. When you struggle with sleeping with your boyfriend or girlfriend, "You are Christ's, and Christ is God's." When you struggle with same-sex attraction, "You are Christ's, and Christ is God's." And when you look in the mirror and desperately want to be someone or something else, remember this: "You are Christ's, and Christ is God's."

Confess your sins. Repent of them—that is, leave them behind. Tell God your struggles. Receive His forgiveness. Your sins, doubts, and struggles don't define you. Here is who you are: "You are Christ's, and Christ is God's."

For you will not be defined on the Last Day by what you aren't. You aren't saved by not being gay. You aren't saved by being straight. You aren't even saved by having all your pronouns worked out with your gender. No, you are saved by Jesus alone. Jesus calls you out of your sins and changes who you are. "You are Christ's, and Christ is God's."

And when others judge you for your struggles, when you judge yourself as you fight through your sins, when the devil whispers that you can't be saved because of your sins, remember whose you are: "You are Christ's, and Christ is God's." That's true of you on the good days when you feel close to God and have everything in your life together. That's most true of you on the bad days when you are a mess of guilt and shame as you struggle with your sins.

"You are Christ's, and Christ is God's." That is who you are in Jesus! You are baptized!

He has made everything beautiful in its time. Also, He has put eternity into man's heart, yet so that he cannot find out what God has done from the beginning to the end.

(Ecclesiastes 3:11)

WHEN GOD CLOSES A DOOR . . .

*Come to Me, all who labor and are heavy
laden, and I will give you rest. Take My
yoke upon you, and learn from Me, for I am
gentle and lowly in heart, and you will find
rest for your souls. For My yoke is easy, and
My burden is light.* (MATTHEW 11:28–30)

Trent was an all-conference basketball player with high
hopes to compete in college and beyond. He led his
team to state last year and was on track to bring home
the championship this year. Several prominent colleges had
already made him full-ride offers.

And then it happened. After jumping up to secure the ball,
he landed awkwardly on his right knee and immediately fell to the
floor. What seemed like a freak accident resulted in a career-ending
knee injury. Just like that, Trent's dreams were shattered, and his
future was filled with more question marks than exclamation points.

In the Bible, we read about a man named Saul. He was a
"Hebrew of Hebrews," blameless under the law and zealous in

his work (Philippians 3:5–6). He was at the top of his class, and his future was bright.

And then it happened. Out of nowhere, he was struck with blindness and became dependent on others to take care of him.

Let's face it. Life can take unexpected turns—and they're not always what we'd choose. Dream-crushing disappointment in life is a reality. A career-ending injury, a college rejection letter, or the fizzle of a meaningful relationship can leave us questioning God and wondering what's next.

What do we do when our plans completely derail?

God used Saul's blindness to profoundly speak to him and radically transform the course of his life. After three days, God sent Ananias to heal Saul and tell him about Jesus. Saul's world changed completely that day, and he quickly started telling other people about his experience.

Saul's new life in Jesus would not be easy. He endured persecution, suffering, and multiple attempts on his life because of his newfound faith in Jesus.

But Saul also had something he didn't previously have: true freedom, contentment, and joy that come only from knowing Christ. He'd later write most of the books in the New Testament, documenting his lifework as God's mouthpiece, proclaiming the Gospel message to the Gentiles. Saul's work and message are a legacy that lives on.

God wrecked Saul's life and put him on a path of purpose. But I'm sure Saul didn't feel that way when he lost his vision and, with it, his independence. At that point, everything seemed to be stripped away from him, and his future was unsure.

Have you heard the saying "When God closes a door, look for a window"? While there's truth to the idea that God directs our steps and can lead us from one opportunity to another, allow me to offer a different version of this saying: "When God closes a door, look up."

Before looking for "the window" or the next opportunity, first look up to God, the One who orchestrates life's steps. Turn to God in prayer, even if—especially if—those prayers are angry shouts or tearful cries. Bring God your shock, disappointment, frustration, and fears. Tell Him everything. He can handle it.

Sometimes, God might send someone into your life to encourage you and help redirect your focus on Him, as Ananias did for Saul. Other times, the person who brings you comfort is Jesus Himself. For Jesus says to you and to me, "Come to Me, all who labor and are heavy laden, and I will give you rest. Take My yoke upon you, and learn from Me, for I am gentle and lowly in heart, and you will find rest for your souls. For My yoke is easy, and My burden is light" (Matthew 11:28–30).

As we release to God what's burdening us, He gives us a new yoke to bear, one that's easy and light.

So, what's next for Trent? I don't know, but God does. As Trent continues to rely on God to take his grief and direct his steps, he can be assured that he'll be exactly where God plans for him to be.

The same is true for you. When disappointment hits hard and knocks you down, look up. Bring your anger and fears to Jesus. In exchange, He promises healing and rest.

But He said to me, "My grace is sufficient for you, for My power is made perfect in weakness." Therefore I will boast all the more gladly of my weaknesses, so that the power of Christ may rest upon me. For the sake of Christ, then, I am content with weaknesses, insults, hardships, persecutions, and calamities. For when I am weak, then I am strong.

(2 Corinthians 12:9–10)

THE FAILURES OF DARWINISM CONCERNING THE HUMAN RACE

D arwinism is not only a theory of biological evolution—it functions also as a worldview. That is to say, Charles Darwin (1809–82) promoted the scientific theory he developed in the 1850s, and to this day, the theory shapes and forms how our society values human beings. Specifically, one of the aspects of Darwin's theory is "survival of the fittest." According to Darwin, only the strongest, smartest, and healthiest survive from one generation to the next, while those who are not as strong, smart, or healthy do not make it. Simply stated, nature is cruel and weeds out genes and attributes that are weak, while the genes and traits that are strong survive and thrive with each proceeding generation.

In one of his writings, Darwin predicted that in some future time the strongest, smartest, and healthiest people would exterminate the lesser, savage people of the world. Now, as previously mentioned, Darwin's scientific theories created and shaped a worldview—his teachings influenced morality and ethics. For example, one does not have to think too hard about this idea to realize that the theory of the survival of the fittest was implemented during World War II by the Nazis. The Nazis tragically placed value on what was called the Aryan race. The Nazis believed the Aryan race was composed of the highest and most supreme human beings in the world. Therefore, anyone not meeting the racial, mental, and physical criteria of the Nazis was expelled from German territory and perhaps even executed at one of their extermination camps.

This proves that theories and ideas can have drastic consequences. But how does this contrast with the Christian worldview?

The way Christians view the world is quite different from Darwin. You see, for the Christian, every human being was originally created in the image of God. From the womb to the deathbed, every life is one that God designed. So no matter how far from the Christian faith our neighbor may be, that neighbor was originally created to be an image-bearer of God. Every person ever born has intrinsic value because he or she was created in the image of and after the likeness of God. You have intrinsic value because you are one for whom Christ died.

The Christian worldview places worth on every person, because every person is one for whom Christ died. That means that everyone around us has worth that is not dependent on physical ability, gender, race, intellect, mental ability, or vocation, but on the fact that he or she is created by the Lord God. Every individual, Christian or pagan, has a Creator and Redeemer. As God's creation, every person needs not only neighborly love, but also the Gospel, that God so loved His created image-bearers that He sent His only-begotten Son, Jesus, to bleed and die for them, to take on all their sin, and to pay the penalty for that sin. People need to hear that Jesus came at just the right time to redeem His beloved creation. Jesus is the sacrifice for all of the people God created—even people who don't believe in Him.

Two different worldviews: one places value on survival of the fittest, and the other places value on everyone created and redeemed by the Lord. One of pushing for power to live in this world; the other one laying down power to give life eternal in the world to come.

THE RACE OF EXPECTATIONS

*Therefore, since we are surrounded by so
great a cloud of witnesses, let us also lay aside
every weight, and sin which clings so closely,
and let us run with endurance the race that
is set before us, looking to Jesus, the founder
and perfecter of our faith, who for the joy
that was set before Him endured the cross,
despising the shame, and is seated at the right
hand of the throne of God.* (HEBREWS 12:1–2)

She crossed the finish line, but she wasn't happy about it. Our cheers and congratulations made no difference to her. I had driven across two states to spend the weekend supporting my friend, who was running her first marathon. She had worked for a year, making plans, meeting with a mentor, and training hard. On the morning of the big race, it was 36 degrees and raining, but she didn't waver. As we dropped her off at the starting line, she was full of determination and energy. When we saw her run past the first checkpoint, she was going strong. But something had changed by mile 21. She was ten minutes behind her pace group, and we could see the disappointment on her face as she ran past. We cheered and shouted encouragement. We even ran alongside her for a block or two, but she didn't smile.

"What's wrong?" I panted, trying to keep up with her.

"I didn't do it."

"You *are* doing it!" I answered. "Your goal was to run a marathon, and you are doing it!"

"No," she said as she turned the corner. "No, it wasn't."

When she crossed the finish line, we congratulated her. She thanked us for our support and smiled for the pictures, but it was obvious that she was devastated. She finished thirteen minutes behind her goal and felt as though she had failed. I didn't understand. She had finished a marathon! To me, that seemed like a huge achievement, but it wasn't good enough for her. It hadn't met her expectations.

What expectations do you put on yourself? If your greatest goals are to achieve, perform, and impress, better get ready for disappointment. If your motivation is to get people to like you, you're running on a rocky road. No matter how smart, talented, or beautiful you are, it will never be enough. The drive to please everyone and meet every expectation will eventually overwhelm you and leave you feeling defeated.

The author of the Book of Hebrews compares life to a race. Hardships and sin slow us down. Guilt and fear make it hard to keep up the pace and move our feet. We can't keep running on our own. We are too weighed down to keep going, let alone finish.

We cannot win the race for acceptance and perfection. Where can we look for help?

Jesus ran the race in a way that you and I never could. He lived a perfect life, yet He took the death penalty for every failure, every flaw of all of mankind. Hebrews 12 says that His motivation was "the joy that was set before Him." His motivation was to see you in heaven! The sure aim of obeying His Father and earning forgiveness for you drove Him to endure the shame and suffering of the cross and hell. Restoring your relationship with God was the goal that kept Him going.

When you discover that you can't meet all the expectations before you and you are worn out with trying, look to the One who finished the race for you. He completed it perfectly. He will carry you across the finish line. Come, share His prize!

Dear Lord Jesus, thank You for finishing the race in a way I never could. Help me to keep my eyes on You instead of on my own failures. Enable me to run with passion and to encourage my fellow runners to focus on the prize You won for us. In Your name I pray. Amen.

NOTHING IS LOST

> *And He who was seated on the throne said,*
> *"Behold, I am making all things new." Also*
> *He said, "Write this down, for these words*
> *are trustworthy and true."* (REVELATION 21:5)

Nothing stays new. When the power of death entered the world, corruption and decay began to take hold.

When we experience illnesses, we miss out on experiences we could have had. A broken bone might make us wonder if our arm, finger, ankle (or whatever) will ever be the same again. A chronic condition (such as asthma) can deprive us of a certain kind of life (one where strong lungs are essential). All these losses can feel like punishments. They destroy dreams.

But that's a gift! Because then we can see the idolatry within the dream. What I wanted was more important than God Himself. In the loss, God is teaching us to bring all our dreams and desires under the petition "Thy will be done." James teaches us to bring every desire captive to the will of God:

Come now, you who say, "Today or tomorrow we will go into such and such a town and spend a year there and trade and make a profit"—yet you do not know what tomorrow will bring. What is your life? For you are a mist that appears for a little time and then vanishes. Instead you ought to say, "If the Lord wills, we will live and do this or that." (James 4:13–15)

The Lord Jesus teaches us not to cling to transitory things. Our treasures can never be kept completely safe: moths and rust destroy; thieves break in and steal (see Matthew 6:19–20).

The same is true with our bodies. Staying alive in this life is uncertain. The only certainty is that we will die, unless Christ returns first. What is certain, however, is that God will give us what we need precisely when we need it.

That is the mystery hidden in the prayer "Give us this day our daily bread." A more literal translation would be "Give us day by day our bread for today." We're asking for what we need today, and God is teaching us to ask not for a lifetime supply all at once but to care for us day by day.

This lesson was taught to the Israelites through the blessing of manna—bread from heaven. God told them He would give them more tomorrow, so take only what they needed for the day. Moses told them, "Let no one leave any of it over till the morning" (Exodus 16:19). There would be more for tomorrow. God will take care of you!

"But they did not listen to Moses. Some left part of the manna till the morning, and it bred worms and stank" (Exodus 16:20).

Gross! God was teaching them a hard but important lesson: "I will take care of you; I will give you what you need when you need it."

Into the fear that we have lost something or will never have something, the Lord Jesus says, "Do not be anxious" (see Matthew 6:25). Nothing is gone that He cannot replace; nothing is lost if we have Him. Although you lose everything in this life, the Lord keeps inviting you to His promise: "I am with you always" (Matthew 28:20).

And then, remember what awaits: "Behold, I am making all things new" (Revelation 21:5). If you are sick, if you feel you've missed out—remember, you haven't lost anything that will not be restored a hundredfold. He is making all things new!

FRIENDS AND NEIGHBORS

*Greater love has no one than this, that someone
lay down his life for his friends. You are My
friends if you do what I command you. No longer
do I call you servants, for the servant does not
know what his master is doing; but I have called
you friends, for all that I have heard from My
Father I have made known to you.* (JOHN 15:13–15)

I like learning the origin of words, their etymology. It's
fascinating. For example, have you ever thought about
how the words **hap**py, **hap**pen, and per**hap**s are related?
It turns out that *hap* is the Old English word for luck. So if
you have good luck, you are happy. Or perhaps things will
go your way if you are lucky. Or if something else happens,
that's just how your luck turned out.

I also like learning different languages and the unique ways
each language teaches its speakers to mentally arrange the world.
So in English, we might say, "She's got him eating out of her hand"
while the French would say, "He obeys her like a dog."

Each language and culture has its own way of approaching the world, which makes it all the more striking when several languages agree on the etymology of a word. This indicates that the idea expressed by that word is deeply rooted in reality.

The word *friend* is like this. Whether it's Greek or English or French or German, the word *friend* derives from "love." In our language, this is somewhat hidden from us since we no longer use the old Germanic word *fron* (meaning "to love"; *frond*, "loved one"). We care for our friends. These are the people we love more than we love the rest of the world. Our friends are special and dear to us.

Here's another word from the Bible that taps into a deep truth of the human condition: *neighbor*. The word *neighbor* has the same etymology in English, Greek, and Hebrew. *Neighbor* is a compound word in English: the boer who is nigh. That is, the farmer who is near you. The guy you share a fence line with. Think of the parable Jesus told when someone asked him, "And who is my neighbor?" (Luke 15:29). After the priest and then the Levite turned away from the man who had been beaten and robbed, the Good Samaritan drew near to help him. God put that poor man in the Samaritan's path, and he did not "un-neighbor" him as the priest and the Levite did. Instead, he accepted the gift God had given him by putting this man near to him. He accepted him as a neighbor. (You can read Jesus' parable in Luke 15:25–37.)

So you have neighbors, and you have friends. You have those people the Lord has put near to you. And you have others you have chosen to be even closer to you: people you have chosen to especially love and care for.

And both are good gifts of the Lord. But noticing how friends and neighbors differ will help you as you navigate the rest of your life. Simply put: God chooses your neighbors; you choose your friends.

Now, of course, your choices can have some impact on who your neighbors are. For example, you can choose where to live. But that's about it. Everybody in that neighborhood is now your neighbor. And if somebody moves away and another moves in, they are your neighbors now. And the people you work with or the other students in your class, they are your neighbors, whether you like them or not. And sometimes, as in the parable of the Good Samaritan, God will just drop somebody right in your path whom you never saw coming in a thousand years. And that's your neighbor too. Everyone the Lord brings you into contact with is someone for you to show the love of Christ to.

Friends are different. They are people you chose based on shared interests, outlooks, values, and a sometimes hard to define just-because-I-like-him.

And here is another thing: friends change over time. Since friendship is based on affinity, your friends will change. You'll lose some and make new ones. Old friends may even hurt or betray you. Or your interests may change, and that means your circle of friends will expand, change, or contract.

Keep your eyes open to this distinction between neighbor and friend. It will help you navigate the world, especially in the coming years when so much will change quickly for you. Choose your friends wisely. Choose faithful Christians you have a lot in common with and whose company you enjoy. And always look for opportunities to show the love of Christ to your neighbors, to all the people the Lord brings near to you.

YOU TOO?

Friendship is built on vulnerability. True relationships aren't developed with shallow small talk and putting our best face forward. We don't build friendships through liking someone's post and curating and filtering our own social media. When we hide our thoughts and feelings, we keep people from knowing us. Authentic friendship that stands the test of time is built on honesty, empathy, and openness.

Friendship can be scary because over time, we must be willing to be open about our failings and trust that we will be given grace. That isn't easy to do. It means sharing what we believe, even if we aren't sure how our friends will respond. Building deep and abiding friendships requires time and willingness to let others learn about us and to trust that they will support us.

It can be especially difficult when friends' beliefs differ from ours. Perhaps they practice another faith or have no faith at all. Perhaps they have grown up in the church but are struggling with doubt and are walking away from the church. These moments can test our ability to be honest, open, and truthful. It is also in these moments when we must trust that the relationship will hold against the strain.

First Peter 3:15 helps us as we struggle through such times. It says, "But in your hearts honor Christ the Lord as holy, always being prepared to make a defense to anyone who asks you for a reason for the hope that is in you; yet do it with gentleness and respect."

We are God's people who reflect the light of the Gospel into the world around us. Our friends know we are Christians, and they look to see what that means in our lives. The choices we make, the words we say, and the priorities we set are ways we show the people around us what God is doing in and through us.

This can leave us particularly vulnerable. Speaking truth and being honest about what we believe sometimes strains a relationship. In those moments, we continue to honor Jesus by sharing both Law and Gospel. We trust that the Holy Spirit will work in those moments to use our actions to increase faith in their hearts. Our part of that doesn't have to be perfect, but it should be filled with warmth, challenge, and grace as we point people back to Jesus.

We can have healthy conversations and discuss earnest questions when we are honest about how we live out our faith. We don't have to shy away from these moments. Instead, we can be confident and prepared to share our hope with others. These conversations can encourage curiosity and uncover places of anger or hurt or misunderstanding. They can even uncover questions we might have.

We are prepared to share our faith with others, but not because we have all the answers. Far from it. We are prepared because God has given us His living and active Word and the Holy Spirit to guide us. We have other Christians and sources, such as the Small Catechism and books like this one to help us. We know teachers and pastors who can answer questions that we can't. Our faith can stand up to good questions and honest conversation because it is based on the truth of God's Word and the power of Christ's Gospel.

The way we honor Jesus in our hearts and defend our hope doesn't come from a place of anger or judgment. That response hurts our friendships and shuts down important conversations. Instead, we are called to use gentleness and respect. As we talk about our faith, we do it with humble confidence.

God is working in us over time and in relationship to share the Gospel. God does the work of growing faith. We can trust in God and approach everyone with love and respect.

Don't be afraid to build true relationships with those who are different from you. The shared moments, vulnerability, and honesty might give you a chance to verbalize the hope you have in Jesus Christ and our salvation through Him alone. With gentleness and respect, we can be good friends to many and share the love of Christ with all.

IN DEED AND IN TRUTH

A few years ago, I moved, and it changed my daily drive to work. Almost every day, I saw men and women on the side of the road who were struggling with a lack of food, housing, and security. My heart broke for them, but I wasn't sure what to do. So, I prayed and did some research. I started keeping plastic bags of nonperishable snacks, socks, and personal hygiene products in my car.

I really don't like speaking to strangers, and I struggle with feeling socially awkward. The first few times I rolled down my window to hand out a bag, I stuttered and felt silly. I struggled with what to say, and once I even thanked the person as I gave him a bag. Then, the more I did it, the easier it got. I gained confidence to ask people their names, if they preferred jerky or peanut butter, or simply to say, "Jesus loves you." I looked them in the eye and then prayed for them as I drove away.

What I do is incredibly small and does nothing to address the underlying needs and systems that cause a person to be in that situation. But every time I hand out a bag, I am reminded of a passage from the Epistle of 1 John 3: "By this we know love, that He laid down His life for us, and we ought to lay down our lives for the brothers. But if anyone has the world's goods and sees his brother in need, yet closes his heart against him, how does God's love abide in him? Little children, let us not love in word or talk but in deed and in truth" (vv. 16–18).

Jesus laid down His life for me and for you. He offered His perfect life so we might be forgiven and receive eternal life through faith in Him. We did nothing to deserve it; it was the most precious and beautiful gift. Jesus' sacrifice shows us just how deeply and profoundly we are loved. We cannot know the depth of God's love and not be changed.

It is easy for our sinful selves to make excuses and judgments. The world is too broken for us to fix, and our small actions won't change anything, or so we think. We believe that keeping our money, resources, and time to ourselves will ensure that no one takes advantage of us. We fear that others will abuse or misuse our generosity. Our hearts can be closed against our neighbors in need.

God's love breaks our hearts for those in need. It calls us to lay down our lives and help our neighbors. We do this not out of obligation but because God's love abides in us. When we act, we do it not for our own glory but to point others to Jesus. The Holy Spirit gives us eyes to see and hearts to use our money, resources, and time to help.

We can and should share the Good News of Jesus through what we say. There is no doubt that we should talk about the baptismal faith we have been given and share the Gospel with others. But it can't stop there. God's love compels us to love in both word and deed. If we believe what we say, our actions should follow.

We can be awkward. We can worry about loving a neighbor in a way that truly helps him because we know true love. We can be generous by helping a friend pay for lunch or by donating to organizations that care for those in the margins or at risk. Even if you don't have money, generosity can be giving of your time to care for people around you. We can do this, confident that every action is a small reflection of the God who has so graciously loved and blessed us.

As God's children, we don't walk past the needs of others. Through the gift of the Holy Spirit, we speak in word and in deed about all God has done for us. Don't be afraid to be kind and to try to meet the needs of people around you. Let God's love abide in you as you love others in His name.

WILL GOD STILL LOVE ME?

Read Proverbs 4:23–27

Read this slowly. Inhale and close your eyes. Exhale, just sit for a minute, and *be*. Be present with yourself—all of you. The good, the bad, and the ugly; the shameful things you've said and done and the things that have been said and done to you. Allow yourself to be in the presence of those things as you and Jesus Christ face them together.

You are not alone. You could never be. In your Baptism, you were joined with Christ. He became such a part of you that whatever you're going through, He goes through it with you. Whatever your sorrow or shame or regret, He feels it as though it were His own. He carries your burden on His shoulders and says, "This is Mine." All for the sake of bringing you back—reconciling you with God.

We all have skeletons in our closets, things we've said and done that we're not proud of. You are not perfect, and you never will be. But the One you're united with and baptized into *is* perfect. You are both sinner and saint—broken yet restored, fallen yet redeemed.

As we spend time with God in mediation on His Word and in self-reflection, we gain perspective about the order He has created. We learn that what He speaks to us, *how* He tells us to order our lives, comes from His detailed knowledge of how we work and operate. I mean, He is the one who sculpted our very lives in the first place. He really does "get us" in all the most relevant ways.

Be. In Him.

> Keep your heart with all vigilance, for from it flow the springs of life. Put away from you crooked speech, and put devious talk far from you. Let your eyes look directly forward, and your gaze be straight before you. Ponder the path of your feet; then all your ways will be sure. Do not swerve to the right or to the left; turn your foot away from evil. (Proverbs 4:23–27)

CHRIST BE MY LEADER

*Rejoice in the Lord always; again
I will say, rejoice.* (PHILIPPIANS 4:4)

Maybe you've seen it before. Maybe you've done it before. It is always special when a young child is allowed to visit a plane's cockpit. The child sits in the pilot's seat, grabs the control column, and pretends to fly the plane. The child proudly occupies the flight deck and imagines what it would be like to actually be in control.

Thankfully, nobody lets the child *fly* the plane.

Imagine if the pilot said, "Hey, kid. Do you want to stop pretending and take this thing for a spin? Here, push this button, and let's see what this plane can do!" People would be sprinting off that plane without their free pretzels.

Like a young child, we often want to sit in the pilot's seat of life. We think we want control. We think we can steer our lives in the best direction without crashing and burning. We often tell God, "I've got this! I'll take control of my life and my plans. I know where I am going. I know what I am doing." Thankfully, God does not let us actually fly the plane of our lives.

God is in control. He steers our lives in the best direction. "And we know that for those who love God all things work together for good, for those who are called according to His purpose" (Romans 8:28). God knows where He is leading you and why He is bringing you to this place.

However, living in this truth can be a challenge. What if you know where you want to go? What if you know what you want to do with your life? If God is in control, does it mean that you have no control?

Unlike the pilot of an airplane, God leaves the cockpit door open. Airline pilots bolt the door shut and offer passengers no access to the flight deck, but God has an open-door policy. In Christ Jesus, you have access to God in prayer. Through the open door of prayer, God promises to hear you: "And this is the confidence that we have toward Him, that if we ask anything according to His will He hears us" (1 John 5:14). God invites you to come to Him in prayer. He wants to hear from you. This means you are welcome to prayerfully make your requests known to God. You may not be flying the plane, but the pilot hears you.

And what if God leads you to a destination you didn't choose? What if God takes your life in a direction that is different from what you expected? That's okay! You can rejoice in the Lord and know that He knows what He is doing. As Jesus hung on the cross dying, it looked like God's plans had gone entirely wrong. The cross looked like exactly the wrong destination for Jesus' life and ministry. Yet, God knew what He was doing. The cross of Jesus was not the final destination. God knew that the cross leads to the empty tomb of Jesus, and the empty tomb means Jesus has overcome sin, death, and the devil for us. The final destination is eternal life with Him.

In Christ Jesus, you can rejoice that you're not in control. That's a good thing! God is in control, and He pilots your life now and for eternity. Your Pilot wants to hear from you and desires your input as to where He leads your life. Still, no matter where He leads you, you can rejoice knowing that God steers your life in the best direction.

For by grace you have been saved through faith. And this is not your own doing; it is the gift of God, not a result of works, so that no one may boast.

(EPHESIANS 2:8–9)

INSIDE AND OUT

Blessed be the God and Father of our Lord
Jesus Christ, who has blessed us in Christ
with every spiritual blessing in the heavenly
places, even as He chose us in Him before the
foundation of the world, that we should be holy
and blameless before Him. (EPHESIANS 1:3–4)

You've definitely had this nightmare before: you arrive at school completely unprepared. Perhaps you are in your pajamas, your hair is a mess, and you haven't brushed your teeth. Perhaps you find yourself at school and you're wearing a towel after having just stepped out of the shower. Or maybe you've dreamed that you ended up at school without any clothing at all.

This nightmare always ends the same way: everyone sees you in this embarrassing situation, talks about you, and laughs at you.

This is one of the most common nightmares. We don't really know what dreams mean, but some believe this kind of nightmare reveals our fear of being seen in a way we don't want to be seen. We want people to see us, but we want them to see only the cleaned-up version of us. We want people to see us as clothed, covered, and confident in our appearance.

The opposite of this—being vulnerable, exposed, and bare—is frightful. We fear that if people saw the real us, they would no longer like us in the same way. We are afraid of what would happen if others could really see us inside and out.

God does see you inside and out. He sees you when you're prepared and put together. He sees you when you're out of sorts and disheveled. God sees you totally, completely, and fully. And He still loves you!

God knows the real you. He knows your hidden thoughts and fears, sins and secrets. God knows your worries and doubts, quirks and oddities. God knows your hopes and dreams, regrets and guilts. He knows it all. He sees you inside and out. While you may have dreams about showing up to school in pajamas or a towel, the reality is that you stand before God completely exposed and unable to hide anything.

And yet God loves you! God chose you in Christ Jesus before the foundation of the world. Knowing all your sins, knowing all your faults, and knowing all your failures—still, God chose you! You are chosen, loved, and forgiven in Christ Jesus.

This means there is no need to try to hide anything from God. You don't need to dress up, get made up, or put up a front before God. You can be real with Him because He already knows the real you. He truly loves you and forgives you, just as His Word declares, "He chose us in Him before the foundation of the world, that we should be holy and blameless before Him" (Ephesians 1:4).

Since you are holy and blameless before God, you can be real with others too. No more fake fronts. No more false facades.

Because God unconditionally loves and accepts you in Christ Jesus, you can be real and honest with others: "If God is for us, who can be against us?" (Romans 8:31). Knowing that you are loved and accepted by God in Christ Jesus puts an end to the recurring nightmare of rejection. God has chosen you and claimed you in the waters of Baptism. Since you are fully clothed in the righteousness of Christ, you don't need to fear what will happen if people see the real you.

GOTTA BREATHE

*For the word of God is living
and active.* (Hebrews 4:12)

Are you a swimmer? Whether you are on a swim team or can only dog paddle, you know the importance of coming up for air. Swimming is hard work. You can have your face underwater for only so long before you have to come to the surface and take a breath. If you want to swim, you've got to breathe.

Of course, it's not just swimmers who need air. It takes almost constant oxygen to keep us humans alive. On average, while at rest, we take a breath every four seconds. That's 900 breaths an hour—21,600 breaths a day! Breathing is repetitive, but it never gets boring. It's the same for other repetitive necessities such as eating, sleeping, and blinking. They don't get old; these things are a vital part of our physical identity. What about our spiritual identity? Sometimes it can feel like our study of the Bible gets old. After all, we've heard the same stories over and again for as long as we can remember. Why keep listening?

We continue to study God's Word for the same reason we continue to take breaths of oxygen: because we need it to keep going. In Scripture, we learn who God is, who we are, and how God interacts with us. Most important, that's where He reveals His plan of salvation in Jesus Christ. These truths define who we are and how we live.

> All Scripture is breathed out by God and profitable for teaching, for reproof, for correction, and for training in righteousness, that the man of God may be complete, equipped for every good work. (2 Timothy 3:16–17)

The devil wants you to forget. He wants you to forget that you are God's loved and forgiven child. He wants you to be so distracted by other things that you don't even realize when you are straying from your faith in Christ. Without constant reminders of God's truth, you can drift from it and find your identity in other things, things that don't last. You may think you've heard all the stories in the Bible, but continuing to study them reminds you of the essential truths that shape your thoughts and actions. Jesus said, "If you abide in My word, you are truly My disciples, and you will know the truth, and the truth will set you free" (John 8:31–32).

The Bible isn't just an old book of good stories and ideas. It is "living and active, sharper than any two-edged sword, piercing to the division of soul and of spirit, of joints and of marrow, and discerning the thoughts and intentions of the heart" (Hebrews 4:12). The Bible is one continuous story that started at creation, traces the lives of God's people for thousands of years, and ends with a sneak peek of events that haven't yet happened. You are a part of this epic story. You stand with God's people: facing hardship, suffering through the results of sin, crying out to God, waiting for a Savior, clinging to hope, and looking forward to the incredible future He has promised in Christ. Your deepest identity is wrapped up in its pages. This is your story.

The Holy Spirit works through Word and Sacraments to keep you strong. Like a lifeline of oxygen, these gifts of the Spirit give you what you need to stay alive. Life is hard work. If you want to keep going, you've got to breathe.

Heavenly Father, thank You for giving me Your living and active Word. Thank You for making me Your child through my Baptism and including me in the epic story of Your people. Continue to work through Your Word to give me what I need to keep going, over and over and over again. In Jesus' name. Amen.

WHEN EVEN THE LATE SERVICE SEEMS TOO EARLY

Read 1 Chronicles 16:28–34

Take a moment and think about the person you would most like to meet. It could be a sports player, political figure, or other influential individual. Now imagine that this person sent you an invitation to join him or her for a meal in two weeks! You're so excited and really in disbelief that your hero would want to meet you, so you rush to check your calendar to see if you're available. You look at the date and realize that you already have an appointment scheduled. You're supposed to get your hair cut that day! So you call your hero with the sad news. She responds, "Really, you're canceling because of a haircut? What about next Monday?" You say, "That's no good either. I need to finish the podcast I'm listening to." Frustrated, your hero tries one more time. "Okay, what about Tuesday?" Again, you're unavailable. "Sorry, I'm going to be really tired from staying up late listening to my podcast, so I'll probably be taking a nap then."

I doubt any of us would actually respond this way. Instead, we would reschedule the haircut, listen to the podcast some other time, and skip the nap in order to tend to a relationship that is much more important than any of those. We make time for the things we value the most or know we need.

Now think about your worship life. Do you make time for worship because it's what you need most? If we're honest with ourselves, this can be a struggle. You may be so busy with sports, work, school, friends, and other activities that you convince yourself that sleeping in on Sunday is better than going to worship. Even if your church has a service that doesn't start until 11:00 a.m., there are many Sundays when even that seems too early. Maybe you don't like the new pastor as much as you liked your previous one, so you don't feel like listening to him. There are no other people your age at church, and you don't feel like sitting with older people. Perhaps you go to a Lutheran school or are active in youth group, so you get your "Jesus time" then. So why do you need to go to the worship service? Or maybe you have to work every weekend. Or you play on, or coach, a select volleyball team that travels every weekend for matches. There are any number of reasons why you may just not feel like going to church.

Here's my encouragement for those times: go anyway! Go and be an active participant in the Divine Service. Even if you think you don't need it, don't have time for it, or have other activities scheduled at the same time, what God offers in the Divine Service is what you truly need. You need His gifts of forgiveness, life, and salvation. You need to hear anew the promises of God for you. God's Word hasn't changed, but you have. Even if it's only been a week since you were in worship, you have changed, so you need to hear again those unchanging promises. You need to be challenged, convicted, taught, and encouraged by God's Word through the liturgy, hymns, Scripture readings, sermon, and prayers. You need to be reminded that this story is not about you but about God as you pray to Him in all things. You need to be encouraged and strengthened by your brothers and sisters in Christ as you meet together, and they need your presence and encouragement as well. The days when you "just don't feel like it" are probably the times when you need God's gifts the most.

The most influential person in your life, in fact, the One who gave you life, *is* inviting you to a Holy Meal, where He will give you what you need to be strengthened in your faith. At His Supper, Jesus gives you Himself, truly present in the bread and wine, with the promise that this is *for you*, for the forgiveness of your sins. What an invitation!

So make time for what you truly need—to be in relationship with your heavenly Father, who has given you everything you need in Jesus Christ. "Oh give thanks to the Lord, for He is good; for His steadfast love endures forever!" (1 Chronicles 16:34).

Fear not, for I am with you;

be not dismayed, for I am your God;

I will strengthen you, I will help you,

I will uphold you with My righteous

right hand. (ISAIAH 41:10)

GRIEVING WITH GRATITUDE

But we do not want you to be uninformed, brothers, about those who are asleep, that you may not grieve as others do who have no hope. For since we believe that Jesus died and rose again, even so, through Jesus, God will bring with Him those who have fallen asleep. (1 THESSALONIANS 4:13-14)

The life we experience as children is deceptive. In the beginning, everything is given to us: food, drink, shelter, clothing. Even luxuries such as toys or tablets are showered upon us. Such is our insanely wealthy society.

Older relatives, such as grandparents, don't discipline us like parents do. They sneak us treats when our parents aren't looking. They spoil us. Life is good, and with them, it's all grace.

In this early life, even pain is temporary. Learning to walk, we stumble and fall. But not for long. We bounce back, become stronger. Cuts and bruises heal. We grow. We feel immortal.

Then, one day, often without warning, unimaginable news arrives. You think, *It can't be true, can it? I've heard of this monster called death but never thought I'd encounter it.*

The death of an older relative is often our first serious experience with the harshness of the fallen world. The feeling of security, even immortality, we felt as children is not the true situation. What is new for us is, in fact, a very old problem: the curse hanging over the world and all mankind. When our first parents rebelled against God's Word, this is what He told them: "By the sweat of your face you shall eat bread, till you return to the ground, for out of it you were taken; for you are dust, and to dust you shall return" (Genesis 3:19).

Psalm 90, the only psalm written by Moses, connects each individual death with the curse of the fall: "You return man to dust and say, 'Return, O children of man!'" (Psalm 90:3). This is a bleak word, but necessary to learn—a person's time in this life is limited. "The years of our life are seventy, or even by reason of strength eighty; yet their span is but toil and trouble; they are soon gone, and we fly away" (v. 10).

In this dark day, in the deaths of those we love, we are reminded that we, together with the whole human race, face the same end. "So teach us to number our days that we may get a heart of wisdom" (v. 12).

The words of Job at the death of his children are often interpreted as stoic strength: "The LORD gave, and the LORD has taken away; blessed be the name of the LORD" (Job 1:21). But stop and reflect on the first three words Job says: "The LORD gave." What I had in this person was a gift. In the midst of grief, try to focus on how God blessed you through your relative. Giving thanks for what God gave, for *who* God gave, honors both the person and God. In remembering the love, advice, acceptance, guidance, and whatever other good things you received, the gift God gave you continues with you. Thank God for how He blessed you, and then ask Him to continue providing for you and ultimately to bless you with the same Christian qualities you saw in your relative.

Finally, remember that we do "not grieve as others do who have no hope" (1 Thessalonians 4:13). We grieve—but as people with hope! We have the hope of the resurrection of the body. When a Christian dies, the soul is with the Lord. And on the day of resurrection, the soul is reunited with a glorified body that will never die. The Christian life is waiting with eager expectation for God to finish the work He has begun. Here is what we wait for: "We await a Savior, the Lord Jesus Christ, who will transform our lowly body to be like His glorious body, by the power that enables Him even to subject all things to Himself" (Philippians 3:20–21).

RELEASED

*If the Son sets you free, you will
be free indeed.* (JOHN 8:36)

You are free! You are free from your sins, free from your failures, free from the things you have done. You have been emancipated from the bondage of death and the power of the devil. You have been released from the prison of sin. The chains of guilt cannot hold you anymore, because Jesus has paid the price for you, has served the sentence of death for you. This is the Gospel!

Sin. You were enslaved to your sins. You were chained to the things you had and hadn't done that were contrary to God's Word. You were handcuffed to the sins you thought weren't that bad and tethered to the sins you couldn't seem to give up.

The worst part of all this is that you need God's Word to tell you how bad the situation really is. You were so enslaved that you deluded yourself into thinking you were maybe kind of good and kind of bad at the same time. Don't bother denying this; I think this of myself too. Sure, we are sinners, but there are far worse people than us. It's not like we aren't *trying* to be better.

God's Word says that we were captive to the religion of this world, the ups and downs of the kind of religion where we deal with God by what we do and don't do for Him and for those around us. We were enslaved to the failed idea that we can make up for our sins by being better and balancing the scales with doing more good than bad. But that kind of thinking just tangles us up even worse. The Gospel truth is that no matter how many times we try to recommit, change, and believe more, we cannot escape Houdini-like from the chains of sin.

Jesus destroyed our prison of sin and death. He was born a human, "made man" as we say in the Creed. He was born to live His life for us. He suffered the punishment for our sins that we deserved. His death on the cross is our death to sin and its aftermath—eternal damnation. He went to hell in our place.

But it didn't end there. His resurrection proves that because Jesus did these things for us, we have forgiveness before God. He now lives and can never die again. In Him, by faith in Him, you will never truly die either. That's because Baptism gave you this new life in Christ. When the water was poured over your head and the pastor spoke the words of Baptism, Jesus redeemed you. He paid the price for you so you would be free from slavery to sin.

You know, of course, that you will live your life on earth, and then one day, you will die. That is frightening for many people. But those who believe what the Bible promises know that physical death means your body will sleep for a little while and, on the Last Day, the Lord will raise it up gloriously. Meanwhile, your spirit will be with the Lord in paradise and you will experience the bliss of being in the presence of God, the angels, and the departed saints. Jesus is at the right hand of God. We, too, are at the right hand of

God, by faith in Jesus. Christ reigns for all eternity and, in Him, we reign too.

His death and resurrection outplays even what you think of you. You stand before God as perfect, just as Jesus does. Sure, right now, you don't feel perfect. Your life doesn't look perfect. You still fight sin with varying degrees of success. But in Jesus—in your Baptism, in the Word, in Holy Communion—you are completely and totally, 100 percent, no doubt about it, holy before God. You are without sin in Christ. This is true on the Last Day when you stand before Him forgiven. It is true, by faith, today.

Here's the best part: you truly are free from your sins! You don't have to live in them anymore. Jesus has broken your chains. That means you don't have to worry about yourself so much, and you can think about other people. You can put their needs before your needs, their wants before your wants, and their going first ahead of you. You don't have to worry about your good outweighing your bad because with Jesus on the scale, everything is going to turn out good for you! He has even rescued you from guilt, despair, doubt, and that nagging feeling that you aren't good enough for God. You aren't! So what? Jesus is!

You are free! You are free from your sins, free from your failures, free from the things you have done. You have been emancipated from bondage to death and the power of the devil. You have been released. No chains or prison hold you anymore.

This is the Gospel! For if the Son has set you free, you are free indeed.

THE GREAT GUN DEBATE AND GOD'S WORD

Do not be conformed to this world, but be transformed by the renewal of your mind, that by testing you may discern what is the will of God, what is good and acceptable and perfect. (Romans 12:2)

A hot topic in the United States is guns. Everyone seems to have an opinion about them.

Considering this, I have felt pressure as a pastor to weigh in on the great gun debate. Now, while I am sure I could offer some helpful insights, I believe it is more important for the church and pastors to speak to the debate from God's Word.

Does God's Word have anything to say about AR-15 rifles or 9mm handguns? No. The Bible, of course, does not mention modern guns. However, God in His Word has a message that needs to be heard—a message that is overlooked.

It is not a message about the Second Amendment or about gun legislation. Rather, it is a message about what is behind gun violence. It is a message that speaks to the human condition—the human heart. You see, a gun operated by a soldier can protect a person from evil, or a gun operated by a terrorist can end the cherished gift of life.

We see this with other things too. Money can bless a family in purchasing Christmas gifts, or it can destroy a family through foolishness at a casino. Prescription drugs can heal an ailment or abuse the body. A knife in the hands of a surgeon can remove a cancerous tumor or, in the hands of an abortionist, can destroy precious babies in the womb. Sex can be a blessed union of husband and wife that procreates a child or a rapist's violation that shatters a person's innocence. That which is meant for good can also be used for evil.

The constant in all these circumstances is not the items mentioned above (guns, money, drugs). It is the human heart. In other words, out of the same heart comes praise and cursing, love and hate, good and evil. Evil is not present in knives, prescription drugs, sex, guns, and so forth. Rather, evil comes from within, from the human heart (see Mark 7:21–23).

Scripture speaks to these problems in our society but does not speak about legislation or what to do about modern material items. It goes much further by showing that the human condition is so lost, so evil, that only a radical confrontation of the sinful heart is sufficient for change. This means that death must happen—death to the sinful nature in Christ crucified.

It is not enough simply to limit or remove items that provide the world with ways to destroy. This would have only surface results, a mere managing of sinful outbursts. Rather, the root of the problem is much, much deeper and needs to be dug out. It is only through the perpetual death of the sinful nature—returning to Baptism in repentance and faith—that there is any hope for reasonable peace, love, and service among mankind. This is much bigger than a gun issue; it is a sin issue.

As the debate over guns continues in our society, steadfast churches armed with God's Word will continue to point out the problem of the sinful heart, the root of all sin. And the Church will continue to call all people to repentance and faith in Christ Jesus, our Lord.

COPING WITH, DISCERNING, AND MANAGING HARD RELATIONSHIPS

Read 1 Thessalonians 1:5–10

In the explanation of the Small Catechism, the very first question is "What is the Christian faith?" The Christian faith is the confession that Jesus Christ is the world's *only* Savior and Redeemer. Believing that and applying it are two very different things.

This life is all about connection. Connection with one another and connection with God the Father through Jesus Christ, who is our only hope. How do we make connections and apply Jesus to people we love in every situation and circumstance? Meeting people where they are, and expecting them to do the same for us, begins at the core of relationship: Human Dignity 101.

The value of human life is not subjective. *Your* value to your Creator is the only unchanging thing in this world. It's not dependent upon circumstances, on how tall or short you are or how good-looking or talented or strong or weak. It doesn't come from race, ethnicity, power, success, or status. It isn't even dependent on your feelings, mistakes, successes, or failures. In the same way that a piece of fine art is valuable because of the artist who created it, your life, all human life, is valuable and irreplaceable because the God of the universe has "knitted [you] together in [your] mother's womb" (Psalm 139:13). When we make the value of a person's life subjective, we give everyone else in the world permission to make that same judgment against us. Understanding this transforms the way we see and approach hard people and situations day to day. God's value of human life is the filter through which we approach every issue we face in life.

Relationships are built on one interaction after another. Each interaction leads us into deeper communication with someone and ultimately results in a relationship of some sort. Meeting people where they are while acknowledging their value in Christ goes a long way toward becoming a relevant voice they'll listen to and respect. If we want to know how to approach other people and how to come alongside them when they're facing struggles or challenges, we have to start by asking ourselves this: Where is *my* focus? What's capturing *my* attention right now, in this moment? And what is it that's causing *me* to see and approach myself the way I do?

Taking time to intentionally nail this down for ourselves is called self-reflection. It's a communication tool we can progressively develop at every age and stage of life. Self-reflection means communicating with yourself to help you figure out what you believe and why you believe it, which then assists you in communicating those beliefs (and sticking to them) as you interact with the world around you.

Self-reflecting teaches you how to see beyond someone else's behavior and into what's captivating their attention at this particular time in life. In 1 Thessalonians, the apostle Paul gives us an incredible picture of what it looks like to be a follower of Christ who not only makes an impact on the culture around him but also is attentive and discerning of what lies or distortions people are buying into. He says that he was among the people of Thessalonica so that they might become imitators of Christ (see 1 Thessalonians 1:5–10).

Our stories, our daily interactions, and building upon one another as we live together are the testimony of our faith. Empathy covers all shame, rage, frustration, confusion, and annoyance. In other words, placing myself in someone else's narrative, looking beyond their actions to their pain, or sharing my vulnerabilities for the purpose of helping them share theirs. This is how we become relevant to one another. This is what opens the door to sharing Jesus—their only hope. They see us receiving Christ and the incredible impact that has on our mentality and perspective. They see for themselves the family of believers we belong to and the identity we cling to as daughters and sons of God the Father.

FINDING IDENTITY

*Before I formed you in the womb
I knew you, and before you were born
I consecrated you; I appointed you a
prophet to the nations.* (JEREMIAH 1:5)

Before anything else, Jeremiah knew whose he was. He may not have known all the implications related to his calling to be God's prophet, but this foundation of his identity was as solid as it could get. He was formed, known, consecrated, and appointed to his identity by God.

Understanding identity today is not that simple. Who we are is fluid—almost to the point of its own confusion. In a quest for freedom and equity, coming to a solid understanding of one's identity is about as secure as nailing Jell-O to the wall.

Right about now, you might wonder how fair it was for Jeremiah's calling to his identity as a prophet of God to have taken place before he could make his own choice on the matter. Was it not an imposition or perhaps even a form of oppression for Jeremiah to have had no choice? Just listen to his response in Jeremiah 1:6:

"Ah, Lord GOD! Behold, I do not know how to speak, for I am only a youth." Does this sound like it was Jeremiah's choice?

God promises in verses 7–10 that He will be with Jeremiah and that He will, in fact, give Jeremiah the words to speak on God's behalf. Jeremiah was going to have some tough messages to deliver. The people might not receive the Word of God, or him for that matter, with kindness. This was a tough identity to be given.

It is popular today to say "to each their own." We not only would prefer to make our own choices, but we also find it terribly offensive to think about taking choices away from anyone else. This is especially true when it comes to gender and sexual preference issues. LGBTQIA+ identity-related issues are everywhere in our culture. Yet, is there an identity even more foundational we ought to consider?

According to 1 Peter 2:9, "You are a chosen race, a royal priesthood, a holy nation, a people for His own possession, that you may proclaim the excellencies of Him who called you out of darkness into His marvelous light." We have a lot to unpack in this verse. To begin with, how can we say that all the various races of people who have read the Bible are together a "chosen race"? What does it mean to be royal, let alone a part of a priesthood? What does a holy nation look like? Certainly not like ours; we have far too many issues. And really, what on earth does it mean to be someone's possession? Are we even supposed to talk like that?

There is a lot here that pushes at our modern sensibilities, but if our thoughts begin with what is central, the whole picture comes into focus. Since much of the talk about identity in our society revolves around love and acceptance, consider God's love for us. Many are familiar with John 3:16: "For God so loved the world, that He gave His only Son, that whoever believes in Him should not perish but have eternal life." Now continue reading verse 17: "For God did not send His Son into the world to condemn the world, but in order that the world might be saved through Him." Jesus Christ came to us out of love. He was not sent to condemn.

Paul reflects on our true identity both before and after our redemption in Christ. He writes in Ephesians 2:1–6:

> And you were dead in the trespasses and sins in which you once walked, following the course of this world, following the prince of the power of the air, the spirit that is now at work in the sons of disobedience—among whom we all once lived in the passions of our flesh, carrying out the desires of the body and the mind, and were by nature children of wrath, like the rest of mankind. But God, being rich in mercy, because of the great love with which He loved us, even when we were dead in our trespasses, made us alive together with Christ—by grace you have been saved—and raised us up with Him and seated us with Him in the heavenly places in Christ Jesus.

In Christ, we are freed from the bondage of sin and made alive to our true identity in Him!

ELECTING JOY OVER JEALOUSY

There is a fable in which the devil travels across the Libyan desert and meets a group of people who are tempting a holy man who was living a modest life alone in a cave. The people try all kinds of temptations, from promising basic human pleasure to introducing doubts and fears. Not one of their efforts is successful. The holy man stands firm. The devil then steps forward and says, "Your methods are too crude. Permit me one moment." Turning to the hermit, he says, "Have you heard the news? Your brother has been made the bishop of Alexandria." According to the fable, the once peaceful face of the holy man becomes disfigured by the stare of hateful jealousy.[3]

The green-eyed monster, jealousy, is indeed dangerous. It destroys relationships and distorts God's creations. In the story above, you have the holy man, who was content and peaceful until he was overcome by jealousy. Jealousy put him into a sorrowful state. He is not alone. The Bible has a long list of people who let jealousy destroy their lives and their relationships with God and others. Paul experienced this in Corinth. The Corinthians were

---

3   P. L. Tan, Encyclopedia of 7700 Illustrations: Signs of the Times (Garland, Tex: Bible Communications, Inc., 1996), 646.

placing a higher level of distinction on preachers and leaders who had helped them in their Christian faith and discipleship. Instead of regarding these men as brothers in their service of Christ, they made them rivals.

> I fed you with milk, not solid food, for you were not ready for it. And even now you are not yet ready, for you are still of the flesh. For while there is jealousy and strife among you, are you not of the flesh and behaving only in a human way? For when one says, "I follow Paul," and another, "I follow Apollos," are you not being merely human? (1 Corinthians 3:2–4)

Here is a who's-who list of victims of the green-eyed monster:

- Cain was jealous of his brother Abel's offering to God, so he killed Abel.

- Jacob and Esau were jealous of each other; they wanted what the other had. Jacob took it too far when he stole Esau's inheritance.

- Saul was so jealous of David that he spent most of his life trying to catch and kill him.

- Joseph's brothers were so jealous of him they wanted to kill him; instead, they sold him into slavery.

- Jacob's two wives, Rachel and Leah, were constantly picking on each other because of jealousy.

- The older brother in Jesus' parable of the prodigal son was consumed by bitterness that his wayward brother was treated with fine gifts and a lavish welcome-home party.

- Two of the apostles rivaled for the top spot among Jesus' followers.

Take a moment to reflect on the people in your life. Are there people you are jealous of because they seem more talented, better looking, or more popular? Have you allowed that jealousy to worm its way into your heart? Jealousy is a powerful emotion that can lead to disaster when it festers.

Instead of being upset over what you think someone else has that you don't have, be joyful for the unique way God created *you*. God gave you gifts that are crafted and designed for you and you alone. When you think about that reality, you are better able to live out your unique calling from God with joy. What's more—you can be absolutely confident that the very best thing God did for you is love you so much that He sent Jesus to be your Savior.

Dear Jesus, it is easy to allow jealousy and feelings of inadequacy to suck the joy and contentment out of me. Fill my heart with joy in Your promise of forgiveness. Give me Your strength, which is made perfect in my weakness. You have overcome the world and its petty jealousies, and You promise to give me grace and peace in my heart. Help me lift up those whose gifts are different from mine. Turn my discouragement into hope and my sadness into joy. You make me complete in You. In Your name I pray. Amen.

THE COMMUNION OF SAINTS

I n the Apostles' Creed, we confess, "I believe . . . in the communion of saints." The word *communion* comes from the Latin word *communio*, which means "to fortify on all sides or strongly" or "a communion, mutual participation."[4] This is what the Lord's Supper is about: together, gathered around the Table, united as the Body of Christ, we fellowship not only with God but also with one another, so that we would be strengthened in faith toward Him and love toward one another. The Lord's Supper is given to the body of believers *together*, and that's what we mean by the "communion of saints."

But it sure is easy to forget that, isn't it? When was the last time you felt left out, isolated, ostracized, or forgotten about? My guess is it's probably pretty recent. Maybe it wasn't a big deal; maybe someone said something nasty about your studies or what you want to do with your life or failed to invite you to something (regardless of whether or not you wanted to go!). Maybe it was a big deal; maybe someone is harassing you at work or school, or

---

4   logeion.uchicago.edu/communio

someone you care about hasn't talked to you in years, or a family member has hurt you deeper than you have the words to say.

We all have someone we miss, someone who has left us or ceased to be the person they were before or died. In this life, relationships will fracture and break from the moment you are born to the moment you die.

But what if those relationships could be made new? Not mended, the way a broken bone ossifies or a deep cut scars, but resurrected?

My home church is designed in the round. While all architectural styles have their strengths and weaknesses, something I really like is that our Communion rail forms a circle around the altar. Circles are symbols of perfection, completion, wholeness, unity, and eternity. Because that's the reality we are made a part of in the Lord's Supper. Sometimes churches have a part of the service called "Sharing of the Peace." Usually, people just sort of shake hands with their pew neighbors, but do you know why we actually share the peace? We are confessing that we are in peace with the other members of the Body of Christ. We do not withhold any forgiveness, nor do we bear any unrepentant sin against them. Why? Because we confess the unity of the Body of Christ—the now-and-eternal Church—when we partake of His holy body and blood in, with, and under the bread and wine in the Sacrament. We are friends, family, all adopted sons and daughters of the Father, equal in our status as redeemed, forgiven children in the eyes of God. Those times you felt ostracized (and those times you ostracized others!) are all forgotten. They're gone! Those relationships are restored, renewed, and resurrected in Christ through the forgiveness of sins.

But it doesn't end there. Not only are you in restored union with those people you see at the rail, but as we sing in "The Church's One Foundation," we are also in "mystic sweet communion With those whose rest is won" (*LSB* 644:5)! You kneel at the rail alongside all those heroes of the faith, all those martyrs of ancient days, all those people you miss, all those whom you never got a chance to say sorry to, and all those who never got a chance to say sorry to you.

Next time you feel left out, next time you feel isolated, next time you feel lonely and heartbroken and cast aside, find peace in this. Your heavenly Father knows you perfectly. Christ Jesus, your Redeemer, forgives you all your sins and knows the pain you daily suffer. Your sanctifying Holy Spirit brings you Christ's good gifts and enlivens you to share them with others. At the Table of our Lord in His Supper, we gather in communion with Him and with one another, redeemed and at peace. Here, you are known and loved by our triune God and by one another. Rest, then, in the communion of saints, this Table of cheer and friendship, this shared cup of joy, blessing, and redemption.

MOUNTAINS AND VALLEYS

*Lord, it is good that we are here. If You wish,
I will make three tents here, one for You and
one for Moses and one for Elijah.* (MATTHEW 17:4)

The Lord does big things on mountains. He gave the Law on Mount Sinai. He showed He was the true God by defeating the prophets of Baal on Mount Carmel. So when Jesus took Peter, James, and John up a mountain, they knew they would literally have a "mountaintop experience"!

Jesus did not disappoint. His body changed! He was transfigured! His clothes became white like light. Moses and Elijah, the big mountain guys from the Old Testament, even showed up to the party and discussed with Jesus His "exodus," which was about to happen in Jerusalem.

Peter wanted the party to continue. Who wouldn't? "Lord, let's set up some tabernacles, tents, for the three of you so we can always be here." But the cloud of God's glory rolled in and shut down the party. God spoke, "This is My beloved Son, with whom I am well pleased; listen to Him" (Matthew 17:5).

The sinners ducked for cover, afraid for their lives. Sinners and God don't mix. God is God, and we are not. What we do and don't do, the sins we commit daily, not only ruin our mountaintop experiences but they also mess up all of our God experiences.

"Don't fear," Jesus said as He touched them. Gone were the cloud, the voice, the Old Testament prophets, and the brightly shining Jesus. They looked and saw only regular Jesus. He took them down from the mountain and turned His face toward another mountain, Calvary, where He would save them for brightly shining God by dying for their sins.

Life is full of mountaintop experiences that feel so real we believe we can practically touch God. We feel so close to Him that we never want those moments to end.

But life isn't lived on top of mountains. We have to come down to the everyday life of homework, jobs, rejection, breakups, sickness, pain, divorce, parents who don't understand us, siblings we wish we could throw off that mountain, and friends who let us down. Life is lived in the valleys and in the trenches, where things don't always shine like the sun and where God seems so very far from us.

But Jesus *is* with you! He's with you on top of the mountain, where things can't get any better, and He is with you, telling you not to fear, in the deepest valley. Both experiences are gifts to you in this life. The mountains and the valleys teach you how to navigate this world, forgiven in Christ. Know, trust, and believe that Jesus went through all the peaks and low places of your universe for you. He is by your side, carrying you through life, bringing you through every moment in order to save you.

Jesus came down the mountain that day and headed for the cross. That shows you something important. You don't really need the mountaintop experiences. They are gifts, but they are not necessary. You already have a gift that's better—what happened at the cross when He got there. You have Jesus' Word and promise. He lived for you. He died for you. He rose for you. He washed your sins away. He feeds you salvation in His Supper.

His life is yours through all times and at every altitude. Jesus' life is yours today in the valley of the shadow of death. It's also yours no matter what happens in all the tomorrows He gives you until the Last Day, when you will see Him shining like the sun for all time. You'll shine on that day too—on His mountain and at His feast, which will never end.

Faith will carry you through all your days and experiences until the end of days. Come soon, Lord Jesus! Amen.

And you shall love the Lord your

God with all your heart and with

all your soul and with all your mind

and with all your strength.

(MARK 12:30)

ANYTHING CAN BECOME AN IDOL

Read Proverbs 3:5–6

You shall have no other gods." This is the First Commandment, and it means "we should fear, love, and trust in God above *all things*" (explanation of the First Commandment, emphasis added). It's easy to trust God with the "generals" of our lives: health, love, provision. But it gets harder when our circumstances seem out of control or too big to handle, when a microscope focuses on the details of those general areas. I'm thinking about what it feels like to be facing the aftermath of casual sex (a pregnancy scare or a sexually transmitted infection, shame, regret) or a person who is battling with the darkness of taking his or her own life. There's so much pressure all around us to be more. It's in the details of our lives where idols creep in and threaten to take the place of our "fearing, loving, and trusting God" in all areas, all circumstances, and amid the everyday, human perceptions of how valuable we are to Him.

Anything can become an idol. The sinful nature of humanity "wants what it wants," and we want it now. Control. In our desperation to be seen and validated, we don't exactly replace God with more instantaneous solutions; rather, we prioritize our lives differently and then agonize over how to get our lives back together. When He tells us in the First Commandment that we "shall have no other gods," it's not coming from a place of demanding that of us; instead, God is coming from a place of understanding. The commandment is a precaution. God is warning us that as sinful, fallen people we will struggle to keep Him as our one true God. He is showing us what it looks like to follow Him and the way to get back on track when we realize we've fallen away.

The First Commandment is about hope. The earthly things we put our faith, love, and trust in will always let us down, but the one true God never does and never will.

There is nothing more comforting to me than knowing that the God of all creation has total control over everything that I do not. And that His entire existence is about being in relationship with me, with each one of us, His pride and joy, through Jesus Christ. We have His attention always, and because of that, we have access not just to continuous stores of hope but also to *the* source of hope amid all things. In Christ, hope never ends.

> Trust in the LORD with all your heart, and do not lean on your own understanding. In all your ways acknowledge Him, and He will make straight your paths. (Proverbs 3:5–6)

YOU ARE THE ONLY YOU

*But now thus says the LORD, He who created
you, O Jacob, He who formed you, O Israel:
"Fear not, for I have redeemed you; I have
called you by name, you are Mine."* (ISAIAH 43:1)

There are nearly eight billion people in the world.

· Roughly four billion of those people are women, and
four billion are men.

· Over seven billion people are right-handed.

· More than four billion people live in Asia.

· Three billion people use the internet or social media.

But there is only one of you!

You are the only you. Out of the eight billion people alive
in the world today, God has made just one of you. You are truly
one of a kind.

Perhaps you don't always feel like you are one of a kind. Maybe you feel like you are just one of the billions of people in the world. After all, there are billions of other young adults. The fact that you are a right-handed internet-user does not make you particularly unique.

And yet, as God says in today's verse, "I have called you by name, you are Mine." You are more than a nameless nobody in the kingdom of God; you are somebody whom God has called and claimed as His very own. At your Baptism, God called you by name and put His name on you. You have been baptized in the name of the Father, the Son, and the Holy Spirit. God knows you by name, calls you by name, and puts His name on you!

Perhaps you have the opposite problem. Rather than feeling like you're just another one of the billions of people out there, maybe you feel like you're the only person in your particular place in life. Perhaps your struggle is finding your place in life and fitting in. You should not be surprised when it's hard to find your place, because nobody else is in your exact place. After all, you are the only you that God has made!

God promises never to leave His people alone. Jesus said, "And behold, I am with you always, to the end of the age" (Matthew 28:20). It's all right if you are having a hard time fitting in. It should not be surprising when it's challenging to find your place in life. Thankfully, you are never alone. God's presence is all around you. He speaks to you through His Holy Word. He hears you when you pray. He comes to you in His very body and blood in Holy Communion. He guides you and is with you through the Holy Spirit.

You are the only you. Out of eight billion people, God has made just one of you. As a child of God, you can have confidence and certainty as you make your way in this world. God called you and put His name on you in the waters of Baptism—giving you identity. God promises never to leave you alone, to be with you always, and to hear your prayers.

Out of eight billion people in this world, God makes this promise to *you*!

AND YET

*For we know that the whole creation has been
groaning together in the pains of childbirth
until now. And not only the creation, but we
ourselves, who have the firstfruits of the Spirit,
groan inwardly as we wait eagerly for adoption
as sons, the redemption of our bodies. For in
this hope we were saved.* (ROMANS 8:22–24)

I've lived in chronic pain since 2015. But when I look back, I realize I've known a life marked by physical ailments and unrest for much longer. Pain of any kind is exhausting and, at times, debilitating. While it's an attack against the physical body, it also wreaks havoc on mental, emotional, and spiritual health, impacting energy levels, school and work involvement, relationships, and a general sense of well-being.

I'm not alone in this. Even for teens, research suggests that about one in every four adolescents (an estimated 20–35 percent) also experiences chronic pain.[5] Even if you don't fall into this

---

5   ncbi.nlm.nih.gov/pmc/articles/PMC5184817/

category, chances are you've experienced unwelcome pain at some point, even if for a moment.

This is not life as God intended. Pain reminds me that I have a broken body in a broken world.

Humans are not alone in this experience of pain. In Romans 8, the apostle Paul writes that all of creation groans together in the pains of childbirth. Nature, too, bears the mark of the fall. Fires devour forests. Tornadoes destroy whole communities. Droughts quell agriculture, livestock, and livelihood. Yes, things are not as they should be.

And yet.

Paul goes on to say that we have the firstfruits of the Spirit. In our Baptism, we were welcomed into God's family and adopted as His children. In Jesus, we find assurance that the pains of our bodies and our world do not get the final say. Our pain will be redeemed. And in this, we set our hope.

Jesus also experienced excruciating physical pain. The Romans were known for their twisted, gruesome mechanisms of torture—crucifixion is one of the most horrific ways to die. In the events leading up to Jesus' death on the cross, He felt thorns piercing His scalp and whips splitting open His back. He endured the crushing weight of rugged wood on open wounds in His shoulders and back and the tear of His own body pulling from the nail wounds in His hands and feet. He knew unquenchable thirst and the struggle of getting air into His lungs as He suffocated. Jesus is no stranger to physical pain.

He's also familiar with emotional and spiritual pain. Jesus was stabbed in the back by a close friend's betrayal. He was rejected by the people of His hometown and unfairly accused and sentenced by the leaders of His own religious organization. He withstood public mockery and bullying when He was already weak and vulnerable. He endured true abandonment by God Himself, by His own Father. Indeed, Jesus understands the weight of pain and bore it in its fullest extent as He hung exposed and battered on the cross until He died.

Then, with His resurrection on the third day, Jesus put an end to pain's power. While we still experience the realities of physical pain, we no longer have to be helpless to them. Jesus' victory over the grave is a victory over pain—physical and otherwise.

Even more, Jesus promises that a day will come when He will bring an end to pain once and for all. We cling to the truth that, in the new creation, we will experience a world where there is no "mourning, nor crying, nor pain anymore, for the former things have passed away" (Revelation 21:4). Behold, Jesus is making all things new, including our bodies.

Until then, we endure our pain with hope. We join with creation in groaning before God. Jesus hears us and knows our pain.

Elsewhere in the New Testament, Paul encourages us not to lose hope:

Though our outer self is wasting away, our inner self is being renewed day by day. For this light momentary affliction is preparing for us an eternal weight of glory beyond all comparison, as we look not to the things that are seen but to the things that are unseen. For the things that are seen are transient, but the things that are unseen are eternal. (2 Corinthians 4:16–18)

So, we wait in hope. Easier said than done? Absolutely. But let our experience of pain remind us that the best is yet to come. Jesus has defeated pain and is preparing for us a new home, where all pain is released.

Come, Lord Jesus, and make it so. Amen.

HOLDING ON AND HOLDING OUT

Read Philippians 4:6–7

W hat is it that you really can't live without? Take a moment to give this some thought, and then ask yourself how many of those things you *really* need. All advertising is geared toward convincing us that we can't possibly live without whatever is being sold. That new phone, streaming service, outdoor experience, collectible comic book—or whatever's on sale this week. All of that is in addition to achievements, family, money, friends, health, and the relationships we can't imagine not having. How am I going to live if I haven't seen that movie (for the fifth time)?

We have this huge list of things we can't imagine living without, and we get anxious when we're missing even one of those things. So, is the solution to anxiety to hold on tighter to what we have? Maybe not, because sometimes the more and more we hold on, the more anxious we become about losing it because we can't imagine life without it. No wonder we're so anxious! We're holding on so tightly to these gifts that we've forgotten about their Giver.

In our reading from Philippians 4, Paul offers a different way of walking through life. He was writing to the Philippian believers, and if anyone had something to worry about, it was the Early Church. They were being persecuted and did not know if they would be able to continue to meet or if they would be killed for their faith. And Paul has the *audacity* to tell these persecuted Christians, "Don't be anxious about *anything*." Don't worry about your church, your family, or your very life! Don't be anxious about *anything*, but in everything by prayer and petition, make your requests to God. Paul's words help us see that we get anxious when we're holding on to the wrong things. We're not meant to hold on to the gifts, but to the Giver of the gifts. We're called to take what God gives us and hold it *out*. Hold it out in prayer and petition, with thanksgiving.

What Paul is calling us to do is to hold on to the promises of God and to hold out whatever is causing us anxiety, fear, and worry. Instead of holding on to our sin, we're called to hold that sin out! Hold it out to our Savior, who takes it upon Himself and gives us forgiveness, restoration, and peace to hold on to instead. We're called to hold out our money and possessions to the Giver of these gifts, with thanksgiving, recognizing that everything we have been given is His! Not 10 percent, not half of it, but 100 percent—it's all Yours, Lord!

We hold our families and friends out to our heavenly Father too, knowing He loves them even more than we do. "Lord, these are Your people! How do You want me to love them, to care for them, and to equip them to share Your message?" When we hold out what God gives us and hold on to His promises, we find we're less worried because *God's got it!*

There will still be times when you hold on to the wrong things. You will try to find your identity, meaning, and value in things or people rather than in God. Here's the amazing truth: this peace that passes all understanding isn't about you holding on to the right thing. The truth is that even as you're holding on to the wrong stuff, God is holding on to you! When Christ held out His hands on the cross, He did so to hold on to you. No matter what you're worried about, whatever causes you anxiety, God is holding on to you today. And He will continue to do that no matter what. He holds us fast, even when we're not holding on to Him.

In a world that is filled with anxiety, you can have peace. Not peace that comes from your bank account, relationships, achievements, or anything else you do or have. You can have peace that comes from your Savior, who holds you fast no matter what. Jesus is the one thing you can't live without, and in Him, you have life now and life eternal. So don't be anxious about anything, but in everything, by prayer and petition, present your requests to God. "And the peace of God, which passes all understanding, will guard your hearts and your minds in Christ Jesus."

WHOSE VOICE CAN I TRUST?

We live in an image-driven world. It is easy to seek approval and even define our value based on the opinions of peers, social media, or our accomplishments. We have to be very careful about placing our self-worth in the opinions of others around us—even people we love and respect, such as parents and teachers and friends. While I understand that tendency and have fallen into that trap way more times than I care to admit, should that be my life goal? Should I always seek the opinions of other people?

A deeper question is this: while considering those opinions, should I allow them to shape my decisions, choices, or define my self-image?

Going even deeper in self-reflection—have I allowed others to taint my view of myself so much that I have lost sight of who God created me to be?

In my life, people have tried to assign labels to me that were not meant to bring out my God-given gifts but to derail God's calling in my life. Some have called me inferior and an underachiever.

People may assign limiting value to you too. That means you have a tough choice. Whose voice will you make a priority?

My prayer for you is that you give priority to the things God says about you as His redeemed child.

Which voice carries more weight? To equip you with God's Word, here are some things the Bible says about your identity. God knows you best because, after all, He created you.

- If you hear others tell you that you are not capable, that there is nothing special about you, the Bible says: "I praise You, for I am fearfully and wonderfully made. Wonderful are Your works; my soul knows it very well" (Psalm 139:14).

- If others say that your very existence was an accident, that you have no real purpose for being in the world, the Bible reminds you: "Listen to me, O coastlands, and give attention, you peoples from afar. The LORD called me from the womb, from the body of my mother He named my name" (Isaiah 49:1).

- If you hear people say you're a lost cause and there is no hope for you, Paul's First Letter to the Corinthians says: "Or do you not know that your body is a temple of the Holy Spirit within you, whom you have from God? You are not your own, for you were bought with a price. So glorify God in your body" (1 Corinthians 6:19–20).

So, just to review, you are fearfully and wonderfully made. From eternity, God had you on His mind. Your Lord and Savior

Jesus Christ valued you so much that He paid the ultimate price to save you. He gave His life as a substitute for yours.

With all that going for you, who would you rather listen to? The voices of those around you who honestly may have other agendas in wanting to keep you down? Or the One who created you, protects you, and redeemed you? I would rather listen to the Creator.

Dear Lord God, I come humbly seeking Your path. I know that faith in You is all I need, but in times when I need clarity, it is so easy to drift away from You. If answers don't come when I want them, I weaken. Still, I know You answer in Your perfect timing. As You teach me patience, calm my mind. Help me seek only You and not rely on my own imperfect solutions or those of others. I'm leaning heavily on You. I give all my anxieties and fears to You. Thank You in the precious name and for the sake of Your Son, Jesus Christ, who took on all my imperfections and makes me whole. Amen.

DON'T LET BIRDS BUILD NESTS IN YOUR HAIR

*Not that I am speaking of being in need,
for I have learned in whatever situation I
am to be content. I know how to be brought
low, and I know how to abound. In any and
every circumstance, I have learned the secret
of facing plenty and hunger, abundance
and need. I can do all things through Him
who strengthens me.* (Philippians 4:11–13)

A common British saying is "You have to take the rough with the smooth"—meaning life will give you good things (smooth) and bad things (rough), so learn to take it all in stride.

That's not bad advice for finding balance in your life. But being a disciple of Jesus is about more than taking things in stride. Each thing that happens to us, good and bad, contains within it a temptation. The good things tempt us to pride. The bad things tempt us to despair. In either case, we measure everything by what pleases us. We make ourselves the center of the universe and so forget the First Commandment. We fear what will hurt us and love what gives us pleasure. We trust in whatever keeps the smooth coming and chases the rough away.

Those thoughts, though, Luther says we should treat like annoying birds. It doesn't "lie within our power to stop them from flying about over our heads. But it does lie within our power to stop them from building nests in our hair."[6]

Learning to persevere through these ups and downs means looking at each thing that happens to you as a little chapter or page in a much larger story. You are on a journey to the kingdom of God. What helps you toward that goal? What hinders you? On a journey, we might get distracted, lose our sense of direction, get injured along the way, stop for refreshment or resupply. We might be delayed because a road is closed or a plane needs mechanical work. But each thing that happens needs to be kept in the perspective of the larger goal. Where am I going? Is this helping me or hurting me from reaching that goal?

The apostle Paul's life changed a lot after he became a Christian. He lost his job, his friends, and his reputation; sometimes, he found himself hungry, chased, and with people trying to kill him. His boat was shipwrecked. He also gained new friends, had adventures, and received food, houses, and money. Paul had a lot of ups and downs. How did he handle it? Whatever he faced, he said, "I can do all things through [Christ] who strengthens me" (Philippians 4:13).

I once saw that Bible verse on one of those inspirational posters. It had a man lifting a heavy barbell above his head. The message

---

6   Martin Luther, *Luther's Works: American Edition*, vol. 13, ed. Jaroslav Pelikan (St. Louis: Concordia Publishing House, 1956), 113.

is that you can accomplish anything you desire if you just have enough faith. However, that is not what the Bible teaches. When Paul says it, he means that whatever came his way, good or bad, he put it in perspective of his relationship to Jesus, his Lord. If he was rich, he saw his riches as a gift from Christ and didn't let it make him greedy and proud. If he was poor, he saw that also as a gift and trusted God to provide him the true riches. The secret, he says, is contentment: "I have learned in whatever situation I am to be content. I know how to be brought low, and I know how to abound. In any and every circumstance, I have learned the secret of facing plenty and hunger, abundance and need. I can do all things through Him who strengthens me" (Philippians 4:11–13).

Whatever happens to you, see it as part of your larger story—your story as a disciple of Jesus. Did you stumble? Give thanks to God that you are still His, and call upon Him in the day of trouble, knowing He will deliver you (see Psalm 50:15). Did you experience a triumph? Give thanks to God that you are still His, give Him the glory, and keep pressing on toward the goal: life in His kingdom!

No temptation has overtaken you

that is not common to man. God

is faithful, and He will not let you

be tempted beyond your ability,

but with the temptation He will

also provide the way of escape,

that you may be able to endure it.

(1 CORINTHIANS 10:1)

ONLY YOU CAN SERVE LIKE YOU

For You formed my inward parts;
You knitted me together in my mother's womb.
I praise You, for I am fearfully and wonderfully made.
Wonderful are Your works;
my soul knows it very well.

(PSALM 139:13–14)

W hat are some words you'd use to describe yourself? Seriously, take thirty seconds to list some in your head! I'll wait here.

What'd you come up with? Maybe you're bold or calm or cheerful or creative or determined.

Our personalities are intertwined with who we are as people. God gave each one of us a personality that is completely unique. Your combination of personality traits makes you different from your sister and your best friend and your dad.

Personality is different from behavior. Your behavior involves the things you do, and your personality is more about who you are. God calls us to behave in certain ways—obey our parents, care for our neighbors, and give glory to Him—but He doesn't command us to have any kind of specific personality. (Not all the disciples were bold like Peter!)

When God created humanity, He didn't create a bunch of robots who would all act the same and perfectly do His bidding. Instead, the earth is full of billions of imperfect people, each with his or her own distinct personality.

Some people are bubbly and outgoing; others are shy and introverted. Your best friend might be goofy, and your cousin might be serious. Maybe your classmate is laid-back, but your sister is organized.

With so many different personality traits, it can be easy to wish you were different. Maybe you wish you were wittier. Less impulsive. More talkative. Less dominant. You might be jealous of someone who has personality traits you want because you think they would make you smarter, more popular, or less awkward.

I know it's hard to hear sometimes, but you are you, and that is a blessing! You might feel that your personality is holding you back, but in reality, it's equipping you to serve in a unique way.

You are loved by a God who knows every aspect of your personality and rejoices when you use your personality to serve Him and His kingdom. Just because your service looks different from someone else's does not mean it's less important.

Your personality is part of your vocation, which is just a fancy word for what you're called to be (like being a student, son or daughter, sister or brother, citizen). People with different personalities can serve in the same vocation, but your personality can help you determine which role you feel called to do!

For example, if you are bold and talkative, you might become a greeter at your church. If you tend to shy away from meeting new people, you might choose to volunteer as a kitchen helper for a community meal. Both of these vocations are important and honor God, but they need people with different personalities.

You don't have to be embarrassed or self-conscious about your personality. And yeah, I know that reading that in a book doesn't really help, but you can be confident in the knowledge that you were created by God for a purpose, and your specific personality helps you serve God and others.

YOUR PHONE AND YOUR FOCUS

> *Do nothing from selfish ambition or conceit,*
> *but in humility count others more significant*
> *than yourselves. Let each of you look not only*
> *to his own interests, but also to the interests*
> *of others. Have this mind among yourselves,*
> *which is yours in Christ Jesus.* (PHILIPPIANS 2:3–5)

You're waiting to be picked up from school, so you absentmindedly scroll through your newsfeed.

You're at a red light, so you quickly check a new text message.

You're between classes, so you catch up on the latest meme your friends have sent.

You see someone walking your way, so you grab your phone to divert your eyes.

You get the idea. Whenever there is a free moment, our hands reach for our phone before our minds even form the thought. We play games, stream videos, and connect with friends. It's fun. It's entertaining. And before we realize it, we can't live without it.

Research suggests that American teens (ages 13–18) use entertainment screen media (not at school or for homework) an average of seven hours and twenty-two minutes each day. The average! That's about the same length of time as the school day. And more than half of teens agree that using social media is often a distraction during times they should be doing homework or paying attention to the people they're with.[7]

Do a quick inventory and consider this. How much time do you spend each day on your phone? (Unsure? Check your screen-time app.) Do you catch yourself not listening to people or zoning out of conversations while considering what's going on between your thumbs? Have you checked your phone while reading this devotion?

Our phones, social media, and virtual connections with friends aren't inherently bad things. But when we crave them more than anything else, we have a problem.

Among other things, a constant attachment to our phones takes us away from being present with the people around us. A phone-obsessed reality is so second nature that we might not even realize the signal we send to our family when we respond to a friend's text at the dinner table instead of answering a parent's question about our day.

What would it look like to live out these words from Philippians 2 through our use of digital media?

> Do nothing from selfish ambition or conceit, but in humility count others more significant than yourselves. Let each of you look not only to his own interests, but also to the interests of others. Have this mind among yourselves, which is yours in Christ Jesus. (Philippians 2:3–5)

7   commonsensemedia.org/research/the-common-sense-census-media-use-by-tweens-and-teens-2019

Considering others more significant than yourselves affects how you engage with the people around you and how you use your time. It could mean putting down the phone to listen to your friend's story rather than playing your favorite game. It could mean honoring your sibling's presence more than your desire to message a friend or watch a video. It definitely means respecting your parents when they ask you a question or put limits on how much time you should spend on your devices.

Looking to another's interests before your own models Jesus, God the Son, who considered our needs above His own so much that He humbled Himself to become a human, a servant. The Giver of life became obedient to the point of death on a cross. Jesus didn't live life by what He wanted to do; rather, He kept us in mind. He lived with His eyes alert and ears open to the needs of those around Him. He was unhurried and stopped to listen to those who called out. He showed compassion and care to others rather than minding His own agenda. And He does the same for you.

In a world where you're constantly bombarded by notifications, Jesus is never too busy to listen to you. He never ignores your questions or spaces out when you tell Him your stories. He is always available to hear your prayers. And He has something to say to you too. It's written in the words of Scripture and proclaimed to you each week at church. Jesus considers you so significant that He willingly went to the cross on your behalf so you could be in a right relationship with God.

As one who knows Jesus, what would it look like to sacrifice some of the time you spend on your phone to care for those around you? Who might God be asking you to reach out to in a meaningful way?

ABUNDANT BLESSING

The thief comes only to steal and kill and destroy. I [Jesus] came that they may have life and have it abundantly. (JOHN 10:10)

Opportunities to view pornography are innumerable. We have access to porn 24/7, all at the click of a button on our phone or other device. Even if we're not searching it out on an explicit site, it can seem like porn seeks us out as we scroll through our favorite social media. If porn is so accessible, can it really be that bad? It's not like we're having sex, right?

Christian and non-Christian scholars alike have studied the devastating effects porn has on the brain. When we view sexually explicit content, our brain releases chemicals that give us feelings of pleasure and enjoyment. This creates a reward circuit encouraging us to view it again and again. Because of porn's addictive nature, a viewer needs to consume more and more, even with increasingly explicit or violent content, to try to reach the same level of enjoyment. As porn rewires the brain, real-life sex can become less stimulating or exciting by comparison. This can damage our bodies and lead to hazardous behaviors.

Not only does porn distort real sex, it can also incite deeper feelings of loneliness, isolation, and depression. That's because porn can't truly satisfy our emotional longing for connection with another human being.

Bottom line: porn is highly addictive and puts real-life relationships in jeopardy. It's not something to be taken lightly despite how easily it can be accessed.

So, where does God fit into all of this?

God created us to enjoy a life of abundant blessing, including sex. After all, He gives the gift of sex and fashions our bodies so it brings pleasure and relational closeness. God knows how incredible sex is, and He gives us rules for how to enjoy it to the fullest.

The Bible defines sex to be experienced within marriage between one man and one woman (Genesis 2:24). Furthermore, Jesus tells us to not commit adultery or even look lustfully at someone outside of marriage (Matthew 5:27–28). Why? Is Jesus a killjoy, trying to withhold pleasure? No, it's actually the opposite. Jesus is telling us how to know and enjoy sexuality through marital intimacy. Jesus' command is given for our good, to keep us from the danger, pain, and despair of misusing God's gifts.

Meanwhile, the devil has always been in the business of tempting people to distort and misuse what God gives us. He wants nothing more than to steal, kill, and destroy that which God has called good. When Adam and Eve had an overflow of abundant blessing living in the Garden of Eden, the devil planted seeds of doubt that God was holding out, that He wasn't giving them the best of all He had to offer. When Adam and Eve explored this further, they discovered the exact opposite was true. When they fell into temptation and ate the fruit God told them not to eat, they discovered shame and fear, not increased knowledge and joy. They learned that the devil is a liar.

We, too, know the shame and fear that come from living life in opposition to what God instructs. We experience the struggle of looking at what we know we shouldn't or doing what we know is wrong. (So does Paul. Check out what he writes about his internal battle in Romans 7:15–20.) And in those moments of shame, fear, and frustration, God comes to us. As He went to Adam and Eve hiding in the garden, God seeks us out, even when we think we can't be found. He speaks our name, calling us His beloved children.

Are there real consequences for sins such as lust and viewing pornography? Yes. But the forgiveness and new life God offers are just as real.

While porn dangerously rewires the brain, the brain can also be retaught. While our sin trashes our ability to enjoy God's gifts, God's grace rebuilds our understanding of what is good. In Jesus, new life is ours, including new sexual lives. While the powers of sin, death, and the devil seek to destroy, Jesus comes to give us abundant life. And that's exactly what He does. Let's trust that Jesus knows what's best for us, even when it comes to our sexual desires. The Author of life has abundant blessings to give.

LOVE VERSUS TRUTH?

*Rather, speaking the truth in love, we are
to grow up in every way into Him who is
the head, into Christ, from whom the whole
body, joined and held together by every joint
with which it is equipped, when each part is
working properly, makes the body grow so that
it builds itself up in love.* (EPHESIANS 4:15–16)

et's start with a simple truth: denominations are a scandal. God doesn't want Christians to be divided. Jesus prays for the unity of those who believe His Word, "that they may all be one" (John 17:21). Earlier, Jesus told His disciples that He is the Good Shepherd, who will gather all disciples into one Church: "So there will be one flock, one shepherd" (John 10:16).

Divisions are caused by human beings either teaching falsely about God's Word or by not loving one another. Often it's a little of both.

The lack of love is a serious problem. Jesus says, "By this all people will know that you are My disciples, if you have love for one another" (John 13:35). At the same time, we are not allowed to pit love and doctrine against each other. There is a temptation to avoid the teachings of Scripture for fear that if there is not agreement, then this will divide. That, however, is not the right approach. In the same prayer where Jesus prayed for the unity of His Church, He also stressed the importance of truth: "Sanctify them in the truth; Your word is truth" (John 17:17). The solution to this is to take these words seriously: "walk in a manner worthy of the calling to which you have been called, with all humility and gentleness, with patience, bearing with one another in love, eager to maintain the unity of the Spirit in the bond of peace" (Ephesians 4:1–3). We don't pit truth and love against each other, but we speak "the truth in love" (see Ephesians 4:15).

It is with great sadness that we realize some people reject the clear Word of God. For example, some churches teach that Baptism doesn't save, even though Scripture says that Baptism "now saves you" (1 Peter 3:21). Some teach that Baptism isn't for children, even though on the Day of Pentecost, Peter called the city of Jerusalem to Baptism, saying, "The promise is for you and for your children" (Acts 2:39). Some teach that in the Lord's Supper, the bread is only a symbol of Jesus' body despite Jesus saying, "This is My body" (Matthew 26:26) and Paul teaching that those who don't discern the Lord's body in Communion are eating to judgment on themselves (see 1 Corinthians 11:29). These kinds of teachings are serious. It isn't loving to say that the words of Jesus don't really matter. Jesus' final instruction in the Gospel of Matthew was to teach His words faithfully (see Matthew 28:20).

In the city of Galatia, some teachers had come into the church there telling people that God's grace wasn't enough for them to be saved; they needed also to follow certain Jewish laws (such as circumcision). Paul called that teaching "a different gospel": "Not that there is another one, but there are some who trouble you and want to distort the gospel of Christ. But even if we or an angel from heaven should preach to you a gospel contrary to the one we preached to you, let him be accursed" (Galatians 1:7–8). Strong words! I'm sure that didn't sound very loving. But to let people believe lies would not be loving.

Different denominations are not just different styles or varieties, like competing hamburger joints. (By the way, so-called nondenominational churches try to avoid the problem by saying they aren't part of any group, but they almost always are Baptist in their theology. Without a church body, the pastor isn't accountable to any church leaders for oversight. That's a dangerous situation and doesn't avoid the problem denominations pose; it only creates new ones.)

Different denominations are ultimately different confessions of what is truth. The most important thing you can do when evaluating a church is look beyond the personality, music, or facility, and ask, "Do you teach what the Word of God teaches? Do you take that seriously?"

Like Luther, I dislike the name *Lutheran*. But I am a Lutheran because I believe that the Small Catechism is faithful to the Word of God. That's the truth.

CUT OUT

*I give them eternal life, and they will never
perish, and no one will snatch them out of My
hand. My Father, who has given them to Me,
is greater than all, and no one is able to snatch
them out of the Father's hand.* (JOHN 10:28–29)

I stood staring at the paper taped to the wall in the school hallway. No matter how many times I read it, I could not find my name. It wasn't there. I hadn't made the cut. I was able to hold back tears until after the bell rang. But once I was alone, they came in a flood.

The school theater meant everything to me. I had been in almost every show since I was a freshman. Looking forward to rehearsals got me through long days of classes and evenings of homework. Drama was my thing. What would I do without it? Who would I be without it?

Maybe theater isn't your thing. Maybe it's soccer, music, or cheerleading. Whatever it is, not making the cut is devastating. It's not just activities either; you can get cut out of relationships too. Having a boyfriend or girlfriend made you feel like you belonged somewhere. Turns out that you liked "belonging" more than you actually liked the other person. Where do you fit after the breakup? Or maybe your gaming buddies stopped inviting you over on Fridays, and you know they are playing without you. Where do you belong now?

It's easy to invest yourself in the activities, relationships, and achievements that make you feel valuable and worthwhile. It's natural to want to spend time and energy doing things that make you feel good. Everyone wants to have a purpose and a place. It's good to enjoy the blessings of relationships, hard work, and fun. They are gifts from God! The danger comes when you allow them to define you. If being "on the team" is the definition of who you are, then who are you when you get cut? If getting good grades makes you feel like you are worth something, what are you worth when you don't achieve?

The multiple forms of rejection you face in this life do not determine your worth. Your friends, parents, teachers, co-workers, teammates, and everyone else in the world can think whatever they want about you—it doesn't change who you are. Your deepest, truest, never-changing identity is that of a loved and accepted child of God. In Christ, you were brought into God's family and included in the epic story of His people. *That's* where you belong. *That's* where you fit in. God considers you highly valuable and incredibly important. He sent His only Son, Jesus, to pay the price for your sins. Jesus faced death for you. You were baptized in His holy, triune name. He earned eternal life for you. Nothing can force you away from Him. No failure or earthly rejection can change your worth.

I give them eternal life, and they will never perish, and no one will snatch them out of My hand. My Father, who has given them to Me, is greater than all, and no one is able to snatch them out of the Father's hand. (John 10:28–29)

In Christ, you have been given an eternal home, a place where you fit in. You can never be *cut out* from where you truly belong.

Dear Lord, strengthen me to face the many forms of rejection I will receive in my life. Help me not to base my identity on things that change. Thank You that no one can ever cut me out of Your love or out of my eternal home with You. Thank You that through Jesus, I will always belong to You. Fill me with the joy and peace that come from knowing I am truly loved and fully accepted. In Jesus' name I pray. Amen.

I have said these things to you,

that in Me you may have peace. In

the world you will have tribulation.

But take heart; I have overcome

the world.

(JOHN 16:33)

FROM THE PAIN OF REJECTION TO GRACIOUS RESTORATION

A few years ago, an angry man rushed through the Rijksmuseum in Amsterdam until he reached Rembrandt's famous painting *Nightwatch*. Before he could be stopped, he took out a knife and repeatedly slashed it. A couple of years before that, a distraught, hostile man slipped into St. Peter's Basilica in Rome with a hammer and smashed Michelangelo's beautiful sculpture *Pietà*. Two cherished works of art were severely damaged. What did museum officials do? Throw them out and forget about them? Absolutely not! The museums hired the best experts, who worked with utmost care to restore the treasures.

One of the foundational grace passages of Scripture is Ephesians 2:8–9: "For by grace you have been saved through faith. And this is not your own doing; it is the gift of God, not a result of works, so that no one may boast."

All rejection is painful. Whether that rejection comes in the form of failed relationships or bad grades, it feels personal. When we are rejected, it feels like someone took God's masterpiece (you) and slashed it with a knife or smashed it with a hammer.

However, like the Rembrandt and Michelangelo masterpieces, we can be restored by grace. Ephesians 2 is one of the most freeing chapters in Scripture. Paul states that God restores fallen humanity by His grace and His grace alone. We play no active role in this restoration; we are passive, on the receiving end. God's grace is a gift. The above illustrations about the famous works of art come into play when we ask why God restores us. Why does it even matter to an all-powerful being? The following verse answers the question:

> For we are His workmanship, created in Christ Jesus for good works, which God prepared beforehand, that we should walk in them. (Ephesians 2:10)

We matter to the Creator because humanity is His crown jewel, His workmanship (or as one translation says, "masterpiece"). God cares because He created every one of us for a unique and divine purpose.

God created us to be perfect, but clearly, we are not. We are slashed and smashed and broken by sin. Satan snuck in and wrecked God's masterpiece. So, what do you do with something unique and valuable when it is broken? You spare no expense to restore it. What did God do to restore His broken masterpieces? He used His one and only expert repairer, Jesus Christ.

Paul reminds us of the repair work of our Savior. "All this is from God, who through Christ reconciled us to Himself and gave us the ministry of reconciliation; that is, in Christ God was reconciling the world to Himself, not counting their trespasses against them, and entrusting to us the message of reconciliation"

(2 Corinthians 5:18–19). Because of what Jesus did for us, we are also in the restoration business.

Dear Father, thank You for loving us so much that You sent Your Son, Jesus Christ, to restore the damage sin has done to Your people. Help us to be ambassadors of restoration. In the precious name of Jesus Christ. Amen.

Be strong and courageous. Do not fear or be in dread of them, for it is the LORD your God who goes with you. He will not leave you or forsake you. (DEUTERONOMY 31:6)

LOSS AND GRIEF, CONFIDENCE AND HOPE

Death was never a part of God's perfect creation. We hear stories of death in the news. We experience the deaths of those we love. As our insides churn, our hearts ache because we know death was never God's design for us. When sin came into the world, God's world was broken. Death became the reality for all living things. Despite our best efforts, no one escapes the impact of death on their lives.

The Bible doesn't shy away from showing us the deep pain that death leaves in its wake. Throughout God's Word, we see faithful people struggle with the reality of loss as they mourn for those they love. One such story comes to us from the Gospels. Siblings Lazarus, Mary, and Martha were followers of Jesus. Jesus had spent time in their home and was their friend.

In John 11, we read that Lazarus becomes sick. Jesus does not rush to Lazarus's side to heal him. Instead, He waits to arrive until after Lazarus has died. When Jesus reaches their home, Mary, Martha, and the whole community are mourning. Martha goes out to Jesus and has a significant conversation about the pain of death and the hope of the resurrection.

Martha approaches Jesus and says, "Lord, if You had been here, my brother would not have died" (v. 21). Brutal honesty. The grief we feel when someone we love dies and our hearts are broken was never what God intended. Regardless of how we were connected or how close we were to someone who dies, death stings. The pain and loss we feel is a recognition of the importance of each person and the absence that is left behind. We don't have to hide that from God. Martha didn't. God can handle our pain. We can go to Him honestly and trust that He will give us love, grace, and forgiveness.

Jesus tells Martha, "Your brother will rise again" (v. 23). Martha says she knows that Lazarus's faith means he will be raised on the Last Day and will spend eternity in God's presence. Even in Martha's sorrow, she is confident that God will make good on His promises. Grief can weigh us down and keep us from reaching out. Yet, we know this earthly life is not the end. God will give us eternal life through faith in Jesus. Our confidence in eternal life can help us to stand when loss weighs us down.

Jesus tells Martha, "I am the resurrection and the life. Whoever believes in Me, though he dies, yet shall he live, and everyone who lives and believes in Me shall never die" (vv. 25–26). Christians put their hope in this promise of Jesus. We don't have to wonder what comes after death. We don't mourn without hope, because death is not the end for those who have faith in Jesus. Even in death, we have confident hope that sees us through the darkest of times.

Grief is a sneaky ninja emotion. It will come for you at the strangest of times, speedy and stealthy and when you don't expect it. You will be happy and laughing one minute and deeply sad the next. Those feelings are totally normal. In fact, even though Jesus knew He would call Lazarus to life and knew Lazarus would live forever in heaven, the Bible says Jesus wept. Grief and loss impacted Him deeply, even though He knew with absolute confidence that Lazarus would not be dead for long.

Death was never part of God's perfect creation. Death is deeply painful, a reminder of our broken state. Jesus knows the pain of losing a friend. Mary and Martha knew the loss of a brother. God can take our honesty and feelings in those moments.

As we mourn, we do so with confidence and hope. Death in our world was not God's intention, but God used the death of Lazarus to show people His glory. God used the death of His only Son to bring us salvation. Because of Jesus' perfect life and death, we can approach death with sadness and grief but also with hope and confidence. Our God makes all things new, just as He did for Lazarus that day. Just as He will for us according to His plan and timing.

RUNNING THE RACE OF RELATIONSHIPS

Read Hebrews 12:1–2

'm not a runner. I've never desired to run a 5K, a half marathon, and certainly not a marathon. However, I would consider running a 100-yard dash to raise money for a charity, as long as those 100 yards were me chasing one of the 5K runners on the last 100 yards to the finish line. That's my kind of race!

Whether or not you're a runner, you know there's a difference between "going for a run" and "running a race." If you're just going for a run, you can go wherever you want, run at your own pace, and choose your own direction. But when you're running a race, you have a course you're supposed to follow, a direction to head in, and a finish line to cross.

When it comes to dating and relationships, I think so many people just run without any real direction. "We're just hanging out." "We don't really want to put a label on it." "Yeah, we might get married someday." "I'm dating him, but I don't think I'll marry him." People use statements like these to describe their relationships as indicators that they're running without clear direction.

Many relationships start as a friendship that turns into something more; however, the more serious a relationship gets, the greater the need for an intentional direction.

Thankfully, God's Word provides us with the direction we need. It even uses the imagery of running a race: "Therefore, since we are surrounded by so great a cloud of witnesses, let us also lay aside every weight, and sin which clings so closely, and let us run with endurance the race that is set before us, looking to Jesus, the founder and perfecter of our faith, who for the joy that was set before Him endured the cross, despising the shame, and is seated at the right hand of the throne of God" (Hebrews 12:1–2). We are called to run, not aimlessly, but to run the race of faith. We often think of the race of faith as running *to* Jesus, as if He's waiting to celebrate with us at the finish line. This view is wrong because it loses sight of the Gospel. The truth is that Jesus not only finishes the race and wins the prize, but He also comes back to give the prize to *you*. His victory is your victory. You are not only running to Jesus, but you are also running *with* Him.

This changes everything, including your relationships with others. Because of Jesus, you have the victory, and you also have a direction for your race: to share this victory in Christ with those around you as you live in obedience to Him.

A dating relationship is meant to follow that direction. This relationship is when two people are individually running the race of faith with Christ, and God brings them together to be running partners. Again, I'm not a runner, but I do know that it's hard to run a race with someone if you're going in different directions. This is why a dating relationship has to have a direction. Where are you headed? Are you both running in obedience with Christ? Do you both know the victory you have in Him?

Too many people think dating is separate from their faith life and are surprised when they are pulled away from the church because they're dating someone who is not a believer or believes differently or is not actively living out his or her faith. Even if your ideal running partner is great to talk to, likes the same music as you, plays the same sport, and says nice things about you, if that person is not running in the same direction as you, none of those things will matter in the end.

The first question you need to ask is, "Are they running in the same direction I am?" Or, to put it more specifically, "Do they believe and live out the same things about God that I do?" Those other characteristics, qualities, and likes come later, but they are not the foundation of a relationship—Christ is. He gives you meaning, value, identity, forgiveness, and eternal life, and you won't find that in any other relationship.

So keep running the race of faith with your Savior, and along the way, look around you at who's going in the same direction. He or she might be someone whom God could bring alongside you. But if not, that's fine, because you are running with Jesus, and He is enough!

BLESSING AND DUTY

*You are the salt of the earth, but if salt has lost its
taste, how shall its saltiness be restored? It is no
longer good for anything except to be thrown out
and trampled under people's feet.*

*You are the light of the world. A city set on a hill
cannot be hidden. Nor do people light a lamp
and put it under a basket, but on a stand, and
it gives light to all in the house. In the same
way, let your light shine before others, so that
they may see your good works and give glory to
your Father who is in heaven.* (MATTHEW 5:13–16)

How can we even count all the blessings the Lord has
given us? The Small Catechism rattles off quite a few in
the explanation of the First Article of the Creed: "body
and soul, eyes, ears, and all my members, my reason and all
my senses." Then, in the section on the Fourth Petition of
the Lord's Prayer, we get another list: "house, home, land,
animals, money, goods . . . good friends, faithful neighbors."

And then there is life and salvation. And from the explanation of the Second Article of the Creed: "[He] has redeemed me, a lost and condemned person, purchased and won me from all sins, from death, and from the power of the devil; not with gold or silver, but with His holy, precious blood and with His innocent suffering and death."

The Lord has blessed us with everything. Our lives, our salvation, our talents, body and soul, time and eternity—it is all a gift from the Lord.

And all this giving from the Lord's hand places a great honor and an awesome duty upon us.

We should not be afraid of duty. We should not be worried about talking about the duties and obligations the Lord has given us. Sometimes we are a bit shy when talking like this for fear of slipping into works-righteousness; if we talk about the duties the Lord has given us, then we might focus too much on that and not on how God has given us life and salvation free of charge for the sake of Christ.

But the Small Catechism is not afraid to talk both about God's giving and our duty in living out what He has given us: "All this He does only out of fatherly, divine goodness and mercy, without any merit or worthiness in me. For all this it is my duty to thank and praise, serve and obey Him" (explanation of the First Article). "That I may be His own and live under Him in His kingdom and serve Him in everlasting righteousness, innocence, and blessedness, just as He is risen from the dead, lives and reigns to all eternity" (explanation of the Second Article).

In the Sermon on the Mount, Jesus expresses our duty by using the images of salt and light. We are called to be the salt of the earth and the light of the world. These images are rich in their connotations.

Salt does more than enhance flavor. It also preserves food by killing off the bacteria that rot food. And salt is also necessary for life: without the sodium ion, our muscles cannot function, and we would die of heart failure. By the way, more than one person has been killed by taking on the dare of drinking a gallon of water in one sitting. That massive intake of water dilutes the salt in the blood and makes it impossible for the heart to function.

Well, you are the salt of the earth. Christians preserve the mercy of God in the world, which defeats Satan, kills sin, and preserves life. We are the bearers of the Word of God. We bring the Good News of Jesus, which alone can add flavor to a world that is worn out by sin and rebellion against God.

And you are the light of the world. Like a prism, you gather the light that is Christ and then reflect that light into every corner. And darkness cannot overcome light. One little light can brighten an entire room that is gloomy and dark. By the power of Christ, which is in you by faith, you lighten the world.

This is a noble duty. Do not be afraid to do it. Do not be afraid to stick out. Do not fear to show your light and to stand out the way a salty sauce stands out when it strikes your palate. It is your sacred honor and duty to be a Christian for all the world to see.

MIRRORS

The LORD sees not as man sees: man looks on the outward appearance, but the LORD looks on the heart. (1 SAMUEL 16:7)

How many mirrors do you have? The one above your bathroom sink, a full-length mirror in the hall, a tiny magnetic one in your locker, the selfie-mode on your phone—seems like we are surrounded by images of ourselves! Depending on the quality of the mirror, you get varying degrees of sharpness. Old mirrors display a cloudy reflection. Dim light makes it hard to see a clear image. Mirrors don't always give an accurate picture of how you really look. Have you ever seen the crazy curved mirrors at amusement parks? They are designed to reflect images with ridiculous distortions. If you judged your appearance based on one of those mirrors, you'd get a totally wrong idea of what you look like. You can't trust the reflections in mirrors like that.

People can be mirrors too. We often measure our worth by the reflection of ourselves we see in others. We let the way people treat us or what others think of us determine what we think of ourselves. It's easy to think that if the cool guy at school said you look weird, then maybe it's true. If your teammates treat you like you aren't worth much, you might start thinking it too. If you judge yourself by what others think about you or how they treat you, you'll get a distorted image of who you really are.

So where can you look to find the truth about yourself? Which mirror is accurate? Beauty comes and goes, skills fade, popularity changes, but your worth does not. Your value comes from the way God sees you. Your unchanging worth isn't based on the many reflections you see and feel. When God looks at you, He sees Jesus. As a baptized, forgiven child of God, you have received the image of Christ. His perfection covers your imperfection. When God looks at you, He sees your heart: a heart redeemed and purified by Christ. By grace through faith in Christ, God sees you as loved, forgiven, and incredibly valuable.

When you define yourself by your eternal value, you can learn to let go of what others say or think about you. You can be who God made you to be, and no longer are you held captive by the opinions of others. What people think of you doesn't make you who you are. God's view of you in Christ makes you who you are.

No matter who you are or what you do, there will be people who don't like you.

No matter who you are or what you do, at times you will feel worthless and not good enough.

No matter who you are or what you do, your heavenly Father stands ready to forgive, love, and fully accept you.

It isn't easy to ignore false reflections and distorted mirrors because you are surrounded by them. They are everywhere. No matter what you see in the mirror, how well you perform, or what others think of you, you are highly valued, completely loved, and fully accepted. When God looks at you, He sees the perfection of Christ. Don't believe the lies.

Dear Lord, help me not to judge myself based on the ways others see me, but on how *You* see me. Enable me to look to You for the truth about my own worth and value. Thank You for sending Jesus to pay the price for my sins. Please work in me to reflect His image. In Jesus' name I pray. Amen.

HYPER-XXX

There is a fable about how to boil a frog. You place the frog in comfortable water and simply increase the temperature of the water so slowly that the frog never realizes the danger all around it. The point is that if you put a frog in boiling water, it will jump out, while the frog in the slowly heating water won't catch on until it is too late.

The temperature has been rising with respect to the sexual temptations in our culture. In 2019, the youngest age at which the majority of students were given a smartphone by their parents was age 11. On the surface, that might sound fine. You may have had a smartphone for several years, and maybe you have exercised wisdom and discretion in using it. However, a recent study noted that 51 percent of eleven- to thirteen-year-olds have seen pornography on their phones. For more than 60 percent of them, their viewing of pornography was not intentional. (The percentage goes up to 66 percent for fourteen- to fifteen-year-olds.)

You may have your phone in your hand right now. With computing power that used to need whole buildings to house, this simple device puts you in connection with much that is beautiful and wonderful in this world, as well as with the corrupting nature of our hyper-sexualized culture. The phone is not the issue. It is merely the conduit through which temptation has access.

Sex is a beautiful thing. God created it, after all. Sex is meant to be enjoyed. That is why God made it truly pleasurable. However, as with much that God made to be good in our lives, sin has raised the temperature of this God-given gift, and we have been less than diligent in watching out for our own safety. The issue is when we give in to temptation and let it dictate our viewing habits, instead of regarding sexuality as an amazing gift from God that should be honored.

God created man and woman to find the other appealing. That we are attracted to one another is not wrong; it is God's design. My grandfather was an artist. In his backyard in Santa Ana, California, he had his own studio where he painted a great many works, one of which caught my eye when I was a young boy. In a field of flowers was a topless woman. I knew this was one of my grandfather's paintings and therefore should have been fine, but I was not sure what to think. So, I asked him. He explained that like the landscapes he painted, he was seeking to capture the beauty of God's creation. I must have had a puzzled look on my face because he went on to explain that as a part of God's creation, the human body is a thing of beauty. The problem for us today is that we have so sexualized the human body that we forget to see the beauty of God's creation in it. The heat has been turned up too high for many of us to be able to see this beauty for what God designed it to be.

Paul reminds us in Philippians 4:8: "Finally, brothers, whatever is true, whatever is honorable, whatever is just, whatever is pure, whatever is lovely, whatever is commendable, if there is any excellence, if there is anything worthy of praise, think about these things."

In Christ, turn down the heat and nurture that which is true, honorable, just, pure, lovely, commendable, excellent, and praiseworthy. In Christ, may the beauty of all of God's creation be restored in our hearts.

NO ESCAPE

*Now Israel loved Joseph more than any other of
his sons, because he was the son of his old age.
And he made him a robe of many colors. But
when his brothers saw that their father loved him
more than all his brothers, they hated him and
could not speak peacefully to him.* (GENESIS 37:3–4)

The Scriptures don't pull any punches when it comes
to the truth about siblings. Family life is anything but
peaceful and tranquil. Consider the following.

Mary and Martha (Luke 10): Martha is the dutiful sister who
does all the chores without even being asked. Meanwhile, Mary
sits around gabbing. Well, that's Martha's version of events. Mary
would say that she was doing the godly thing by listening to Jesus,
while Martha was trying to get her in trouble by tattling on her:
"Mary's just sitting here, while I do all the work!"

Joseph and his brothers (Genesis 37–50): Dad has his favorite,
and all his brothers hate him for it. But they also hate him because
he's got a pretty high opinion of himself and isn't afraid to brag.

(Why else would you tell your brothers you had a dream that they would all bow down to you one day?)

David's children (2 Samuel 15–1 Kings 1): Where to begin here? Jealousy, anger, assault, rebellion, murder . . .

Jacob and Esau (Genesis 25): Jacob is bookish; Esau is an outdoorsman. These twins have no common interests. They can't stand each other's presence. Jacob is embarrassed to have such a hick for a brother, and Esau can't stand being associated with such a wimp. How are they even related?

We haven't even touched on stepsiblings yet—or, trickiest of all, only-children trying to navigate a world of people who have these weird relationships they've never experienced. It turns out you can't escape siblings even by never having one!

All of these biblical stories increase in poignancy as you grow older. I had a brother growing up. Then I acquired a stepbrother and two stepsisters. Then I married a woman who has two brothers and a sister of her own. And now I watch my own children (some boys and some girls) relive all the old mistakes, sins, and pitfalls that I lived through. It doesn't matter that I've seen it all before. I'm doomed to see it all again in their lives.

The human condition doesn't change. Human nature has been the same since Adam and Eve fell into sin. So a bunch of sinners living together in a household keep on doing what they have always done. This is why old literature still resonates: nothing has changed in the human heart since Macbeth, or even since Cain and Abel.

So isn't it a bit odd that the New Testament says that all of us Christians are brothers? Who wants that? Who would choose to have siblings when they're nothing but trouble?

But again—the trouble is not out there in the siblings. The trouble is right here in my heart and yours. If you were all alone on a desert island, you'd still find a way to sin: complaining, feeling sorry for yourself, neglecting your prayers. In your heart of hearts, you know very well that you'd find a way to sin even with nobody else around.

So God gives us siblings, both in our family and in the Church, as a gift—a many-faceted gift. Siblings are mirrors in which we can see our own failings and learn to repent of them. And siblings are our nearest neighbors, whom we can learn to serve as the Lord has served us.

Don't forget: Jesus is our Brother. We are adopted into the family of the Father only because Jesus has made Himself our Brother. We inherit the Kingdom because it rightfully belongs to Him, the firstborn of creation and the only-begotten Son of the Father. And each of us, equally, stands in need of this grace and mercy. Each of us is equally a brother in Christ, a sibling for whom the Lord died. It is a lifelong journey to learn that lesson in humility. If you were blessed enough to have siblings in your home, then you got a jump start on learning it.

May the God of hope fill you with

all joy and peace in believing, so

that by the power of the Holy

Spirit you may abound in hope.

(ROMANS 15:13)

GEORGE BORGHARDT

THE REAL PROBLEM

*Take heart, My son; your sins
are forgiven.* (MATTHEW 9:2)

The paralytic couldn't walk. He was helpless. His entire
life happened on his mat. He was stuck there. He was
even carried around on it. That was his problem—he
was paralyzingly stuck on his mat.

But Jesus sees the paralytic's real problem—his sins. His
sins separated him from God and from his neighbors. His sins
weren't the direct cause of his being stuck on that mat, but sin is
the cause of all sickness and death in this world. Sin is *the* problem.

Sin is your problem too. Sin cripples your vertical relationship
with God and messes up your horizontal relationships with those
around you. Big sins, little sins, sins that bother you, sins that
don't—all of them mess up your relationships. All your failures,
all your doubts, all the evil you do, and all the good you don't
do have their source in your doing (or not doing) what you want
to do instead of what God in His Word has told you. It probably
doesn't land you paralyzed on a mat. No, far worse! It will land
you directly in hell.

Sin is also the problem of your neighbors. They don't do what they should do, and it hurts you. And they do what they shouldn't do, and it hurts you. Big hurts, little hurts, pain so great that you can't even look at them—and sometimes it can feel like you'll never get over what they have done.

The cross. That's the solution to the paralytic's sins, your sins, and your neighbors' sins. All sins were answered for on the cross of Jesus. His perfect life and His bitter sufferings and death are the final word for the sins of the world. He died for our sins, and He was raised for our forgiveness (Romans 4:25).

Forgiveness! Jesus forgives all your sins. He delivers forgiveness to you over and over again. He washed your sins away at the baptismal font. He speaks forgiveness in your ears through the preached, read, and absolved-upon-you Word. He feeds forgiveness to you in Jesus' body and blood, given for you to eat and drink. Forgiveness, given for all your sins. Forgiveness, delivered for every sin that you have done, are doing, and will do. You are completely and totally forgiven in Christ.

Your neighbor is also forgiven by Jesus. All his or her past, present, and future sins were answered for by the same Jesus who answered for your past, present, and future sins. That means the sins he or she has done, is doing, and will do against you are forgiven by Jesus. And if He has forgiven the sins committed by others against you, how can you withhold forgiveness from them?

What if they aren't sorry? Well, consider how Jesus is toward you. He forgives your sins, sometimes even before you know they are sins. He is merciful to you and absolves you of sins while you are still working through them. His forgiveness enlivens you to live for Him. Could He do that for your neighbor too?

"But, I can't," you say. I know you can't. He also knows you can't. That's why He forgives them first, before you do! Forgiveness isn't yours anyway—it's His forgiveness. In other words, you forgive others with Jesus' forgiveness.

So start by asking God to forgive those terrible sins you can't forget. Ask Him to help you repent. After all, who are you to withhold forgiveness from others? Who are you to say that Christ died to forgive all sins, *except* that other person's sins? And while you're at it, pray for God to bring about repentance in your neighbor too.

And when you doubt Jesus' forgiveness, remember the paralytic on the mat. Jesus looks at the unbelieving people around Him and says, "Which is easier? For Me to forgive this man or heal him?" So they would know—so *you* would know—that Jesus has the authority to forgive sin, He told the paralytic to take his mat and go home. And the man did just that!

You do too, you know. You leave your sins, take your mat, and go home—forgiven. And if you are forgiven, then so is everyone around you. Forgiveness, earned by Jesus on the cross and delivered to you. Forgiveness, delivered to you and given to others.

Cheer up! Your sins are forgiven! Your neighbors' sins are too!

LOVE YOUR ONLINE NEIGHBOR TOO

Screenshot. New message. Select image. Type: "Did you see this?"

It's a familiar story. Maybe the screenshot was of a post on social media. A private text. A secret shared in a self-destructing message.

Or what about this? You're walking around school and see someone trip and something embarrassing falls out of her bag. You stumble across two people doing something they shouldn't in a hidden corner of the hallway. You overhear a story about that party last weekend. Or what about those countless people you encounter every day who are wearing a weird outfit, have an unflattering haircut, showing off an ugly tattoo, or are just obnoxious? You snap a pic. You take a video. You retell it over text, in a tweet, on Snapchat.

It happened in public, so it's fair game, right? It's not lying, right? You're just telling other people about it because it was funny or because they ought to know about it, right?

How would you feel if someone was secretly taking pictures or videos of you? Slyly texting all their friends about something foolish or bad that you did? Announcing your absolute worst moment to all their followers? Or, what about the people whose mortifying moments you share? What if they saw what you texted, tweeted, or snapped? What if they saw those pictures and videos? Would they still want to hang out with you, talk with you, be your friend? Would they feel betrayed? Would they be confused as to how you could do these things and still call yourself a Christian?

You know about the Eighth Commandment, right? "You shall not give false testimony against your neighbor." What does this mean? "We should fear and love God so that we do not tell lies about our neighbor, betray him, slander him, or hurt his reputation, but defend him, speak well of him, and explain everything in the kindest way" (explanation of the Eighth Commandment).

Martin Luther takes it a step further in the Large Catechism:

> Here belongs particularly the detestable, shameful vice of speaking behind a person's back and slandering, to which the devil spurs us on, and of which much could be said. For it is a common evil plague that everyone prefers hearing evil more than hearing good about his neighbor. We ourselves are so bad that we cannot allow anyone to say anything bad about us. Everyone would much prefer that all the world should speak of him in glowing terms. Yet we cannot bear that the best is spoken about others. (LC I 264)

People slandered their neighbor in Reformation times. People slandered Jesus during His earthly ministry too. When Jesus was betrayed by Judas and then appeared before Caiaphas, the high priest, and the Pharisees, Matthew writes: "Now the chief priests and the whole council were seeking false testimony against Jesus that they might put Him to death, but they found none, though many false witnesses came forward" (Matthew 26:59–60).

But it wasn't just the Pharisees' slander that nailed Jesus to the cross. It was yours. Because of your sin—your lying, your gossip, your mean-spirited texting and posting—God the Son had to die, bloody, betrayed, and alone. He took all that onto Himself. He became the slanderous gossip and the backstabbing friend. For you. Jesus, true God and true man, true friend for *you*, took your sin-filled self and reputation and exchanged it for His sinless one. Your sin has been paid for, atoned for by Christ's death. Your heart of stone has been swapped out for a heart of flesh (Ezekiel 36:26), and now, freed from sin, you are freed to love your neighbor.

So repent and turn from your gossip! Stop taking those screenshots, stop sending those texts. Luther writes:

> I can indeed see and hear that my neighbor sins. But I have no command to report it to others. Now, if I rush in, judging and passing sentence, I fall into a sin that is greater than his. But if you know about it, do nothing other than turn your ears into a grave and cover it, until you are appointed to be judge and to punish by virtue of your office. (LC I 266)

Guard your neighbor's reputation like you hope she guards yours. Speak kindly of your friends—and your enemies! Love your neighbor, online and off.

UNFILTERED, UNEDITED, UNCROPPED, YET STILL LOVED BY JESUS!

He must increase, but I must decrease. (JOHN 3:30)

By changing just one letter, Facebook becomes Fakebook. You've probably heard that one before.

The world of social media is an edited version of real life. Don't like your complexion in a picture? Filter it. Don't like the lighting on your clothes? Edit it. Don't like the other person in the picture? Crop it.

Once we have thoroughly filtered, edited, and cropped our photo, it's time to release it into the wild for others to vote on it with their likes and favorites. If we get lots of likes, then we must be likable. If we don't, then the whole world sees that we are lacking in likability.

Behind our preoccupation with social media is our longing to be liked and valued by someone else. We desperately want not only to be liked but also loved.

The Good News of Christ Jesus is exactly that: God does not just like you, He loves you. God has not just given you a thumbs-up from far away. Rather, He has given His very life for you on the cross. We get caught up in whether people like us enough to click a tiny, heart-shaped button; meanwhile, God has enough heart for us to give His very life for us on the cross.

Even more, Jesus did not die for the filtered, edited, and cropped version of you. Rather, Jesus willingly died for the unfiltered, unedited, and uncropped you: "but God shows His love for us in that while we were still sinners, Christ died for us" (Romans 5:8). Despite your sin, Jesus gave His life for you. His suffering and death on the cross and His resurrection from the dead on the third day is proof that God not only likes you—He loves you!

The love of Jesus profoundly changes how we interact with social media. Unlike the rest of the world, we do not need to obsess over our likability. Since we know that we have been eternally favorited by God in Christ Jesus, we can stop puffing ourselves up on social media. Loved by Jesus, we do not need to endlessly filter, edit, and crop. Loved by Jesus, we can use social media in more constructive ways. We can use it to point others to our faith in the love of Jesus.

John the Baptist was not talking about social media, of course, but we can learn something from his words in our verse above: "He must increase, but I must decrease." John was talking about Jesus. Rather than putting the spotlight on ourselves so that we increase in likability, we can use social media in a way that reveals Jesus to others. Before posting something on social media, first ask, "Does this reveal the love of Jesus?" If not, edit or delete and try again.

God has done far more than just click a heart-shaped button to show His love for you. Rather, God's heart for you compelled Him to send His Son to die for you. Jesus faced the cross and the devil and left the tomb empty out of love for you. There is nothing fake about the love of Jesus!

Do not be anxious about anything, but in everything by prayer and supplication with thanksgiving let your requests be made known to God. And the peace of God, which surpasses all understanding, will guard your hearts and your minds in Christ Jesus. (PHILIPPIANS 4:6–7)

YOU ARE MORE THAN A PHYSICAL BODY

Read Galatians 5:16–25

Temptation is a frustrating and confusing animal. It lingers and messes with our minds. It lures us into its tunnel vision and threatens to distort the way we see and approach ourselves. The only way to make it stop is to give in to it or change the subject away from it. (Which, depending on how that goes, will lead us either right back into the temptation or, preferably, drive us to make choices toward a healthier, more peaceful lifestyle.) The thing about temptation is that it feels good for a little while. The initial payoff can leave us with the impression that we've found a solution to the problems and cravings we're up against. But in the same way that sugar cravings don't stop after eating one candy bar, temptations have far more intricate effects on the way we see and approach ourselves: our identity, our sexuality, our relationships, and our overall value to this world.

Here's what you need to know: *sin* is tempting, and temptation is Satan's oldest trick in the book. In Genesis 3, the first words he ever spoke to mankind were to tempt Eve into sin, distracting her from the good life she had with God, separating her from the identity she so clearly saw when she was in His presence, and creating chaos in a life built on community with God and the world around her.

Although we might not realize this until it's pointed out to us, Satan and a casual-sex culture have become steady whisperers in our ears, pointing us to see our sexuality as the place where our identity is found, *where we'll finally feel like we belong to someone or something* and feel that who we are is *enough*. We look to sex and our sexuality as the means of defining who we are and why our existence matters. Unfortunately, this mentality doesn't end at the altar when two people say "I do" on their wedding day any more than it ends after a hookup or even a sexual relationship outside of marriage.

The Sixth Commandment, "You shall not commit adultery," reminds us that we should "fear and love God so that we lead a sexually pure and decent life in what we say and do, and husband and wife love and honor each other" (explanation of the Sixth Commandment). Why is this good and right and beneficial to us at all ages and stages of life? Because when we are in the presence of Jesus, we see the value of every person's life much more clearly. We see that humankind is God's most priceless possession. Everything He does and says is for our benefit; He knows the timeless tricks Satan uses to distract, confuse, separate, and isolate us. When sexuality is turned into anything other than what God created it to be—whether that is casual sex outside of marriage, homosexuality, pornography, self-pleasure, sensuality—it might feel good and right and beneficial at first, but this is a temptation. It's a temptation to defile the valuable creation you are. It is Satan's mocking of what matters most to almighty God. Left uncared for, sin and temptation threaten to separate us from one another and, ultimately, separate us from Jesus, our lifeline to getting through this life.

We need Him. Together, with your husband or wife, the powerful connection of sexuality creates all *good* things that draw you closer in relationship with each other, closer with the family you'll create and grow together, and it gives the clearest picture of what true love is meant to be.

WHAT DOES IT MEAN TO BE TOLERANT?

I f there is a primary value in American culture today, it involves tolerance. No one likes to be thought of, let alone called, sexist or racist. A variety of "ists" and "isms" have been declared inappropriate for the modern person to be associated with. The question remains, however—just what does it mean to be tolerant?

Would you say that you are tolerant of your parents? Well, maybe. You might tolerate their decisions if you don't agree with them, especially if they keep you from doing something you very much want to do. Yet, would it make sense to say you are tolerant of your parents if you agreed with them?

I am a fan of the Angels, not the Dodgers. It would make little sense for me to say that I tolerate my sons being Angels fans themselves. Nor would it make sense to say that I tolerate them playing on Little League teams that are called the Angels. On the other hand, when my son was on the Dodgers in Little League, *that* I had to tolerate. While I wear an Angels hat with pride to my sons' games as Angels, I could not bring myself to buy a Dodgers hat. I did not cheer any more or less in either situation, but I did have to tolerate my son in a Dodgers jersey.

How might this apply to how we tolerate others in today's cultural climate? We are expected to tolerate other religions and people with sexual preferences or gender identities that do not match their biological identity. Implied with this expectation is that we do not offer disagreement. This does not logically work. If the expectation is to not disagree, then there is no need to tolerate because it makes little sense to tolerate what we do not disagree with.

But before I get overly logical and sound cold or close-minded, what we ought to do as Christians is to emphasize inclusion. Inclusion does not mean overlooking or ignoring our differences or disagreements, but rather seeking to include even those with whom we have disagreements in our lives, that the love of Christ may be shared through us to them. This has long been a Christian value that should continue to shape how we approach those with whom we have differences.

Paul in Galatians 3:27–29 writes:

For as many of you as were baptized into Christ have put on Christ. There is neither Jew nor Greek, there is neither slave nor free, there is no male and female, for you are all one in Christ Jesus. And if you are Christ's, then you are Abraham's offspring, heirs according to promise.

This does not mean that there are no longer races, ethnicities, or genders. It does mean that in Christ, all these identifiers are bound together. This is a restoration of the unity we already have as children of God. All humanity is made in the image of God and is due respect as such. Thus our non-Christian neighbors are all deserving of inclusion and true tolerance.

As our neighbors, all those people God places around us are worthy of our love because He created them and loves them. We might not agree with how and who they worship, and we may discuss our differing beliefs with them, but this is done respectfully. Tolerance and inclusion mean allowing for differences because of our unity as children of God in our common humanity. By listening respectfully to our neighbors, we are equipped by the Holy Spirit to bring the truth of the Gospel to them, shining the light of Christ at just the right places in their lives.

THE DOUBLE-EDGED SWORD OF BEING ONE OF A KIND

You are one of a kind.

Did you read that sentence as a compliment or an insult? We have all heard those words, or ones like them, spoken in affirmation when someone does something extraordinary or is exactly the right person for the task in front of them. We have also heard the words used in anger, stinging with rejection, as someone is seen as too different, too hard to understand, unable to fit in with others. The same six words, yet context and inflection give them dramatically different meanings.

There is truth in that sentence. God's Word tells us that God has lovingly formed each of us. Yet, being one of a kind, just like that sentence, can be a double-edged sword.

You are uniquely created by God. Isaiah 43:1 says, "Thus says the Lord, He who created you, O Jacob, He who formed you, O Israel: 'Fear not, for I have redeemed you; I have called you by name, you are Mine.'" You are created and formed by our all-powerful God. This same God has called you by name and redeemed you through Jesus' death on the cross. You are one of a kind, a person created and known by God.

You are one of a kind. No one has your same gifts, skills, passions, and experiences. We can spend a lot of time criticizing our appearance, our gifts, and our status. The truth is that God made you and placed you with great intention. You aren't an accident or a mistake. In your Baptism, God has given you important ways to serve the church, your family, and your community. Other people need you to be exactly who God has made you to be. God's world is richer for having you in it. The Body of Christ benefits when God works in and through you.

Being who God made you and baptized you to be is not easy. In fact, it can be desperately difficult and even lonely at times. If we are true to who God made us to be and to the faith He has given us, we might discover we don't fit into the world the way others do. Living as Christians in this world can be difficult. We have God's Holy Spirit to help us love our enemy and to protect all life as precious. God calls us to be light of the world and a city set on a hill (see Matthew 5:14 from Jesus' Sermon on the Mount). This doesn't mean we get to fit in or blend in with the crowd. In fact, it makes us stand out.

You are one of a kind, someone who doesn't just blend in with the world. Isaiah 43:2 reminds us that waters, rivers, fire, and flame will threaten us. The world will sometimes feel dangerous. It will be overwhelming, and we may even wonder where God is. We are going to experience rejection and loneliness. Yet God promises that He will be with us every step of the way. God will protect us and support us with His Holy Spirit.

You are one of a kind, but you are never alone. You have a God who loves you enough to send His only Son, Jesus, to die for you. That same God walks beside you through everything and gives you a community of Christians who share your faith. God has given you faithful people who love and care for you, even in times when you feel alone.

You are one of a kind, and that can be both wonderful and difficult. In those times when it is a joy, we celebrate. We praise the God who made us and called us by name into faith. When it is hard, we remember Isaiah 43:4: "Because you are precious in My eyes, and honored, and I love you." You are loved deeply by God. When there seems to be no one else quite like you, remember that as a Christian, you are going to be different. When loneliness and rejection set in, remember that you are loved by the one true God, and He has given us one another to be the Church together.

You are one of a kind; never doubt it. It is exactly how God made you to be.

SERVING GOD BY SERVING OTHERS

When I was in high school, the very last thing I wanted to do was be a church worker. My parents were both Lutheran teachers. I had seen that life and wanted something else for myself. For a time, I worked as a janitor during my breaks from school. I also got a job with a friend's father, who had a business doing taxes for church workers. That seemed more interesting. Taking accounting classes in high school made good sense, so later, off to college I went.

By that time, I had met a couple of DCEs (directors of Christian education) who had spoken into my life and opened the door to considering church work. I started college with the idea of double majoring in business and ministry. But in my first tax accounting course, I learned that my passion was not numbers, but people.

That is just a glimpse of my own vocational journey, one I still travel today. You are just beginning that journey. You may have a specific concept of what you would like to do for a profession, or you may wonder what jobs will still exist in thirty to forty years. Can I introduce a concept that may push your thinking a bit? The concept is *vocation*, a word not always well understood.

In the Medieval Church of Martin Luther's day, to have a vocation was to be called to ministry as a priest, monk, or nun.

Luther taught an expanded definition to help understand vocation as it relates to our relationship to both God and to people. Rather than seeing vocation as merely being called to join a monastic order as Luther himself had, he came to see that it is not God who needs our service but our fellow man.

One way to consider this is to think about a pair of images the Bible uses concerning faith and service. The first is the image of the vine and the branches in John 15. Verse 5 is the key verse, where Jesus explains: "I am the vine; you are the branches. Whoever abides in Me and I in him, he it is that bears much fruit, for apart from Me you can do nothing." If we see this as our work, this image strikes us as a requirement for us to produce fruit. However, taking a closer look at the text, notice that it is by abiding (remaining) in Christ that fruit is produced through us, the branches, by Jesus, the vine. Just think how odd it would look if a branch disconnected from the vine produced fruit. It's not natural. What is natural is the branches having fruit produced through them by the vine.

The second image is the body. Paul uses this image in Romans 12 and in 1 Corinthians 12. By considering our unity as the Church as a body, Paul is helping us to understand how we are able to depend upon one another. The way we are made in Christ forms us for our unique service as a part of the Body of Christ, the Church.

I was not formed to prepare taxes but to serve as a DCE. God has wired me with a passion for the spiritual care of children, youth, and families. To seek a job outside that vocational calling would make little sense. But beyond just where I work, this shaping has placed me in other vocations that reflect Christ's image in me. The most important of those other vocations for which God has shaped me are those of husband and father. Every way that I, as a part of the Body of Christ, serve others is a part of my vocational calling.

As you look for ways that God has gifted you to serve the Body of Christ, seek the ways you find joy in the service. God has created you to be who you are in Christ. In whatever vocations God places you, put that to good use serving others in the name of Christ.

Trust in the LORD with all your heart,

and do not lean on your own understanding.

In all your ways acknowledge Him,

and He will make straight your paths.

(PROVERBS 3:5–6)

THE QUESTIONS YOU DREAD

When I was a senior in high school, I remember everyone asking me the same two questions: Where are you going to college? What are you going to study? I grew to dread those questions because I didn't have an answer for either one. No college or career choice was clear to me. I knew some of my gifts, skills, and passions, but I couldn't find a direction or get pointed toward a particular achievement like my peers.

The pressure around these questions has only grown since I was in school. In a recent study, members of Generation Z (Gen Z— those born between 1996 and 2010) were asked to complete this sentence: "My (fill in the blank) is very important to my sense of self." The number one answer was my "professional and educational achievements."[8] You are a part of a generation that is ambitious, innovative, and driven to succeed. Many of those around you feel pressure to be the best, to focus on accomplishment, and to work hard toward a goal or a career.

As others drive toward goals, achievement, and success, you, too, might dread questions about your future. Frustration

---

8   *Gen Z: The Culture, Beliefs and Motivations Shaping the Next Generation* (Ventura, Calif.: Barna Group, 2018).

and anxiety can cloud your vision of the future and sneak into your day-to-day thoughts. You might struggle with knowing your gifts, skills, and passions or how you want to use them. Maybe you have tried to choose a direction but worry your choice will disappoint you, your family, or even God. It can feel like people are watching as you stand still in the middle of a racecourse, while everyone else runs past.

When we struggle to know the future and set our goals, we can look to God's living and active Word. Read Ephesians 3:8–10, and remember these two things:

First, God's love does not depend on our goals, achievements, college choice, or future career. We have been saved by grace through faith, not because of anything we have done. We can't boast about saving ourselves. We did nothing to earn it. God's deep and abiding love sent Jesus to the cross to forgive our sins and ensure that we spend eternity with Him. We are dearly loved children of God, His workmanship. Nothing we do or don't do will change His love for us.

Second, God can and does use us, no matter where we go or what we do. God prepared things for us to do long before we were born. We have vocations, and they aren't something we have to choose or figure out. Vocation is a calling, through our Baptism, to unique roles and tasks through which God cares for His creation. It doesn't depend on you, the right college choice, grades, or making sure your team wins. You have vocations right now in your church, family, school, team, and community to share God's love in word and deed. God gives vocations, and He works through you to accomplish them.

The wonderful thing about vocations is that they never go away. You have vocations now as sibling, child, student, citizen, worker, neighbor, and more. Those roles and tasks can change and grow as you move through life. If you don't know what career you want to pursue or how you want to dedicate your time, that's okay. No matter what you do, God will use your gifts, skills, and passions to be His hands and feet in the world.

As you approach graduation and other big transitions in life, you will always have questions about your future. But you don't have to dread the questions or the answers. You can be confident in God's love and forgiveness for you. Your identity as God's child never changes. Regardless of what the future holds, God is going to use you to love and care for the people around you.

If the future seems too much, focus on your vocation right now, today. Look how God will use you to care for His creation and point others to Jesus. Goals, plans, and achievements can wait. Focus on who you are in Christ, and use what you have been given to love the people around you in His name.

ONLY TWO TYPES OF PEOPLE?

've heard it said there are only two types of people: those who know they are sinners, and those who do not know they are sinners. Those who know they are sinners confess their sins with repentance. Those who do not know they are sinners conceal and celebrate their sins as though they are fine.

Every single person in this world breaks one of two ways. Either we lower our head in repentance, or we raise our chin with pride. But the fact remains that no one is good, not even one. Every single person falls short of the glory of God.

So how do we live as Christians with this understanding that there are only two types of people? Well, for starters, we must understand that we are no better than anyone else. We are all equally beggars in need of God's grace, but some people don't know it yet. Second, we do not need to compete to prove we are the best and greatest. As Christians, we need not go through life consumed with the need to accumulate as many trophies as we can or to do better than our friends. And third, as Christians, we do not continually look at ourselves as the center of the universe (because we certainly are not).

Now, the reason all of this is true is because you receive the gift of Christ's forgiveness. Jesus is the One who descended to the cross to defeat death and rise from the grave for you. This means that Christ is not only the center of the universe but the reason why you are free from the need to step on top of people or to put them down to make yourself number one.

As a Christian, you have Christ, which means you can selflessly love those around you, even your enemies. You need not be continually looking to climb the ladder or fixate on yourself because Christ has come to you and made you His own.

So, no matter how messed up a friend or neighbor may be, we recognize that he or she is a sinner just like us, and we *all* need Jesus. We acknowledge that we are no better than they are, except that they may not have Christ. This means that we are in a remarkable place not only to love them as fellow people created in the image of God but also to confess and tell them about the gifts of Jesus that are for us *and* them. It can also be said that there are only two types of people in this world: those who know they are forgiven for Christ's sake and those who have yet to hear that wonderful news.

WELLNESS IS A SKILL THAT CAN BE LEARNED

Read Psalm 139

"You are what you eat." Think for a moment about the power that food has on our entire body—physically, mentally, emotionally, socially, and even spiritually. The food we eat determines our physical growth and nourishment. It can either contribute to or inhibit neurological responses in the brain. Weddings, funerals, graduations, birthdays, promotions . . . all of these focus around eating and drinking with family, friends, and co-workers. Even emotionally—what are those comfort foods that make us feel better when we've had a rough day? Chocolate? Ice cream? Popcorn with extra butter? Without a doubt, what we choose to subject our bodies to will contribute, if not determine, our overall well-being and the actual worldview to which we eventually subscribe.

It's not just cookies and fast food we need to be aware of if we want to have a happy, healthy, safe, strong, and faithful future. It's the mental, emotional, social, and spiritual food we choose to consume that will affect us as well. You are not just a physical body needing physical nourishment, but as Psalm 139 awesomely shows, we are physical bodies who think things, feel things, and are in relationship with God and with people around us.

The five intricate areas of our life mentioned at the beginning of this devotion require balance. Like spokes on a wheel, each contributes to propelling the vehicle forward. When one or more are weakened or broken, we have to slow down, take a close look at each spoke, and take the time to get it fixed so we can move forward again.

With this knowledge and the wisdom found in the First Article of the Apostles' Creed, "I believe in God, the Father Almighty, Maker of heaven and earth," we have powerful and tangible guidance for finding happiness and gratefulness and hope and purpose over and over and over again, no matter what sin or the devil throws our way. "I believe that God has made me and all creatures; that He has given me my body and soul, eyes, ears, and all my members, my reason and all my senses, and still takes care of them" (explanation of the First Article).

Meditate on ways you can fix a broken or weakened physiological "spoke." Here are some thoughts to get you started:

· *Physical Spoke*: Am I eating fresh, unrefined foods such as fruits, vegetables, and meat or other protein? Am I giving my body opportunities to breathe fresh air and release "good mood" endorphins each day by being outside and walking, running, playing? (Yes, playing!)

· *Mental Spoke*: Am I communicating my thoughts in a way that feels comfortable to me, such as journaling, songwriting, storytelling, poetry? Am I able to use those avenues of communication to build deeper connections with people around me? Can I share them to encourage someone else who might be going through the same thing I am?

· *Emotional Spoke*: Am I using my creativity to express my emotions in healthy and consistent ways? God gave us art: playing an instrument, singing, writing, drawing, painting, dancing, building—all types of creating—for the purpose of expressing our feelings when words aren't enough. Art helps us balance our emotional spokes.

· *Social Spoke*: Am I making time to be with the people I love? Sometimes, this means being the one to pull the family together when everyone is going in different directions. Am I making it a priority to be in church and Bible study with the brothers and sisters of my Christian family, even if my biological family isn't present? Am I surrounding myself with people who affirm the value of every human life, who honor their own life and that of others?

· *Spiritual Spoke*: Am I reading my Bible? Am I hearing the Word spoken to me? (Faith comes by *hearing* the Word of God.) Am I recalling my Baptism, when I was joined together with Christ and made a member of

His eternal family? In the Sacrament of His Supper, am I eating His body, which strengthens, cleanses, and restores my body? Am I drinking His blood, which gives me all I need to face another day?

We are all sinners in need of a Savior. Thank You, Jesus, for the open invitation to share my life with You: my sins, failings, challenges, and successes. Thank You, Lord, for Your forgiveness, which gives me a big sigh of relief and reassurance to face tomorrow.

WHAT MAKES YOU *YOU*

But the serpent said to the woman, "You will not surely die. For God knows that when you eat of it your eyes will be opened, and you will be like God, knowing good and evil." (Genesis 3:4–5)

Some ideas are best expressed in poetry. To get at other ideas, the novel is the proper form of literature. For example, some of my favorite novels are about friendship and the inner workings of the human mind. You can both teach and learn more about such things in the pages of a novel than you can in an essay on friendship or a scientific paper on brain function.

And when it comes to philosophy, the hard work of convincing people how to live and what is best in life is no longer done by wandering sages such as Socrates, standing in the marketplaces asking questions of passersby. Who reads Plato or Aquinas or Wittgenstein these days anyway? If you want a truly influential philosophy of the human condition, you go to the movies. And not just any movies. The movies that deal with (dare I say "preach"?) our culture's philosophy of the human condition are sci-fi movies.

Think about it. The question is this: What makes us human? What is valuable about human beings?

Now think about any sci-fi movie.

- *The Matrix*. Choose the red pill or the blue pill. Your choice will determine everything.

- *Minority Report*. The precogs can see the future and know who will commit crimes before they happen. Is our hero really doomed to commit the crime he sees, or does he have a choice?

- *Avatar*. It is within your power to choose which side you want to be on; you can even choose to move from one species to another.

- *Interstellar*. Humanity can choose its own future, even what planet it wants to live on.

- *Blade Runner*. Are the AI robots truly human? What would make them so? Do they have free will to choose?

I could go on and on, but this gets boring. In fact, I kind of feel bad about pointing this out to you because now you'll be able to guess the basic outline of any sci-fi plot in the first fifteen minutes of the movie. The message is always clear and always the same: free choice is what makes humans human; to choose is the essence of what is good about humanity.

And now you also know why those who don't value human life in the womb call their position "pro-choice" instead of "pro-abortion" or "pro-termination of pregnancy."

What a shallow philosophy this is! The mere fact that you can choose between choice A and choice B is what makes us human? The mere ability to decide? My cat can decide whether he wants soft food or dry food for lunch. He simply refuses to eat what he doesn't want and makes a ruckus until somebody gets him what he does want. I'll give you this much: the ability to choose is part of animal life, certainly a prerequisite for reason and anything that can be called thinking. But to say that this is the summation of what makes humankind human is an embarrassingly shallow statement.

No, it's worse than that: it's a satanically shallow statement. Satan said to Adam and Eve, "Don't follow the Lord. Make your own way. Choose your own path. That will make you like gods. The ability to choose your own future—that's what's worthwhile."

Nonsense. What is worthwhile is *choosing what is good*. What makes humankind human is following the Lord, who created humanity. We cannot truly be ourselves unless we act in accordance with the plan of Him who created us. To truly know ourselves, we must know the Lord. To truly live, we must follow Him who created life and who is life itself.

God is life. God is love. God is good. Therefore, to choose Him is to choose life and love and goodness. And to turn away from God is, therefore, death and hatred and evil. The choice is necessary, but it is the thing chosen that makes for happiness or sorrow, life or death.

Think of how many times in the New Testament Jesus is tempted to walk away from the Father's plan. If You are the Son of God, turn these stones into bread. If You are the Son of God, come down now from the cross, and we will believe in You.

Satan presents Jesus a choice also. But Jesus knows that He can be the Son only by choosing rightly, not merely by choosing.

And thanks be to God. Jesus has chosen you within the Father's plan of salvation. That's what makes you worthwhile. That's what gives value to all human life, from the womb to the tomb.

BEING SENT

Read 1 Peter 2:9–10

What are you going to be when you grow up?" We ask this question so frequently, especially of high schoolers. But I don't think it's a great question. It is asking you to find your identity in your job or what you do. You are going to college to get a degree in teaching so you can *be* a teacher. You're studying for a law degree so you can *be* a lawyer. You're joining the military so you can *be* a soldier. Or you're getting an English degree so you can be . . . English. 'Ello Gov'na!

"What are you going to *be*" is a question of identity. Answering that question with what you *do* is the wrong answer because they really are two different questions: "who are you?" and "what do you do?" Thankfully, God's Word answers both questions:

> But you are a chosen race, a royal priesthood, a holy nation, a people for His own possession, that you may proclaim the excellencies of Him who called you out of darkness into His marvelous light. (1 Peter 2:9)

The first part of this verse tells you who you are: chosen by God, made holy because of Jesus, and precious to Him. That is who you are! That is your identity, and it is separate from what you do (also known as your vocation), in the sense that what you do doesn't impact who you are in Christ. Serving as a pastor or church worker doesn't make you more loved or chosen by God than any other job. A mechanic is just as forgiven as a stay-at-home mom or dad. Your identity comes from God—you are loved, forgiven, and chosen by Him because of Jesus! That's who you are! This is good news because if you lose your job, change your major, get injured in your sport, or experience any other change in your life, it doesn't impact your identity and value.

This is important because so many young people leave high school hoping to find their identity. What I want you to see and understand is that you already have your identity; it is given to you in Christ. You're not going to college or to the workforce to *find* your identity, but to live it out. You're loved by God, and He has given you gifts and talents so you can, as our verse says, "proclaim the excellencies of Him who called you out of darkness into His marvelous light." You are a witness to the Gospel, an ambassador of the King of kings, and you can use your gifts to do that in many vocations. What matters more than what you do is whether you're a faithful witness to God while you're doing it. Wherever you end up after high school, make sure you find a place where you will be reminded of who you are. Get involved in campus ministry at your college or get to know your military chaplain. Above all else, find a local congregation that you will call home, where you will be reminded of who you are and where you will receive God's gifts in the Sacrament.

What am I going to be when I grow up? Here's a snapshot of what your answer to that question could be right now: I'm going to be a child of God. I will continue to be imperfect but saved by a holy and perfect God. I will be loved by Him, not because of my performance but because of Christ. That's what I'm going to *be* when I grow up, no matter where I end up. Now, what am I going to do? That I haven't figured out yet, and it may change over time. But I do know that whatever I do and wherever I go, I am being sent. I am being sent on a journey not to find my identity but to tell others about the One who gives me my identity. I am being sent as an ambassador of the King of kings to love and serve His people using the gifts He has given me. I am being sent not for my own glory but for His. I am being sent not to go it alone but to be connected to His Church wherever I am. I am being sent for more than getting grades, serving well, or earning a paycheck. I'm being sent to make a difference in the name of Jesus, and I can do that faithfully wherever I go because Christ is with me wherever I go.

SELFISH?

"Which commandment is the most important of all?"

Jesus answered: "The most important is, 'Hear, O Israel: The Lord our God, the Lord is one. **And you shall love the Lord your God with all your heart and with all your soul and with all your mind and with all your strength.'** *The second is this: 'You shall love your neighbor as yourself.' There is no other commandment greater than these."* (MARK 12:28–31, EMPHASIS ADDED)

hen was the last time you flew on a plane? If you paid attention to the flight attendant's speech before takeoff, you heard something like this: "In the event of an emergency, oxygen masks will fall from the ceiling. Please secure your own oxygen mask before helping those around you." The first time I heard that, I was surprised and a little shocked. After all, shouldn't I help others first? It sounded selfish to put my own well-being above that of others. Why in the world would they announce such a selfish rule?

Of course, the answer was obvious. I would need to wear the oxygen mask because I couldn't help anyone if I were dead!

When Jesus was asked which of the commandments is the most important, His answer wasn't what the crowd expected. He said that we are to love God first and love others second. Does it seem surprising that Jesus puts greater value on your relationship with God than on your relationship with others?

The most important thing in your life is your relationship with God. Nurturing the faith God gave you at your Baptism is your highest priority. Without your connection to God, you won't have the strength to help others. He fuels your acts of service. Investing time in the cultivation of your own faith and taking care of your own spiritual well-being isn't selfish.

God values your whole self. Your body, your mind, and your emotions are gifts from Him. Taking care of your health isn't putting yourself first; rather, it's being a good steward of what the Lord has given you. Making wise choices when it comes to caring for your physical health is part of valuing God's gift of your body. Talking about your feelings and getting help when you are overwhelmed is an aspect of caring for your emotional well-being. It may seem selfish to spend time and energy on self-care, but when you are in a healthy state of mind and body, you are better able to serve others.

The Lord serves you the spiritual oxygen needed to live and the spiritual food needed to thrive. His Word is life-giving oxygen. When you receive the body and blood of Christ, you are given spiritual food for sustenance. God gives you His forgiveness in a way that is so real you can taste it!

There are many exciting ways to stay connected to God's Word and grow in your relationship with Him. You can breathe it in during personal devotions, group Bible studies, gathering together for worship, meditating on a Bible verse each day, remembering the gifts of Baptism, memorizing Scripture—the list goes on and on. Focusing on your relationship with God isn't selfish. It's essential.

Heavenly Father, thank You for giving me my body, my mind, and my emotions. Please enable me to make wise choices to care for them and to be a good steward of my own health. Most of all, thank You for sending Jesus to restore my relationship with You. Thank You for giving me faith in You; please help me to cultivate that gift! Thank You for nourishing me through Your Word and Sacraments. All this I bring to You in Jesus' name. Amen.

THEY WILL TOSS YOU OUT

*I have said all these things to you to keep
you from falling away. They will put you
out of the synagogues.* (JOHN 16:1–2)

The Bible I had for confirmation class was one of those fancy ones with red letters for the words that Jesus Himself spoke during His earthly ministry. I sometimes wonder if that's a good idea—it might actually give us the impression that *only* those words in red count, as though the rest of the Bible is not really the Word of God. That's nonsense, of course. Our Lord inspired the entire Scripture from Genesis to Revelation. But one advantage of the red-letter Bible is that you can see at a glance all the times Jesus sat His disciples down for a good long talk. And that's certainly an interesting thing to think about. What are the topics Jesus spent time on with the disciples? What did He want to make sure they understood?

If you flip through a red-letter Bible, you'll find things such as the Sermon on the Mount (three chapters of Matthew) or the Olivet Discourse (Mark 13). The Sermon on the Mount covers a lot of ground, so no surprise that it's lengthy. And the Olivet Discourse is about the end times, so again, no surprise. But if you turn to John's Gospel, the longest discussion you'll find is an intimate portrait of Jesus' time with His disciples leading up to His crucifixion. In chapters 12–16, Jesus prepares His disciples for what it will be like after He is arrested, after He gives up His life on the cross, after He is risen from the dead.

This conversation is the longest string of red letters you'll find in the New Testament, and it's about one thing: preparing the disciples to live in a world that is hostile to Jesus.

Jesus warns the disciples that the world won't like them. If the world didn't listen to Jesus, then it won't listen to Jesus' followers either. Therefore, the disciples should expect trouble. They should be prepared for rejection. They should not be surprised or disheartened when people ignore them or are even hostile to them.

Jesus sums up His warning by telling the disciples: "They will put you out of the synagogues." What does that mean? It means that the disciples will be rejected by their community. Their friends will turn their backs on them. Their own family members will disown them. The people they do business with will cut them off. They will be ridiculed. Others will laugh at them. They will be looked down on and made fun of. They will be cut off and alone.

That's what Jesus wants His disciples to be ready for. It's bad enough to have those things happen, but it would be even worse if such things came as a surprise and caught them off guard. So Jesus spends a long time talking to His disciples about this in John 15 and 16.

You should be ready for this too. We live in a society that has turned its back on the Lord. Those who steer our culture hate the Lord Jesus. This is what the Small Catechism is talking about when it says our enemies are the devil, the world, and the flesh. The world is oriented away from God. Whether it's the music industry, influencers on social media, the news media—the overwhelming message of our culture is anti-biblical. What would Instagram be without lust? Doesn't it strike you as odd that the news, which is supposed to report what happens, actually drives a narrative ("love is love," abortion "rights," etc.)?

So listen to Jesus' warning. The world does not love the Lord Jesus. Do not be surprised by this. It will get no better as you grow older. There will be more and more pressure from those around you to abandon your faith, to stop going to worship, to give up praying, to ignore the Bible.

Will you be intimidated by all this pressure, or will you follow Jesus, who warned you ahead of time that all this would happen? Will you trust a culture that wants you to be nothing but a consumer, or will you trust the One who allowed Himself to be consumed by death on the cross for your sake?

TRADING WORRY FOR GODLY COURAGE

am guilty of being a world champion worrier. I ran across this quote one day, and it has stuck with me: "Worriers spend a lot of time shoveling smoke."

For many reasons, it is hard to have an unwavering trust in God. The primary reason is that Satan works hard to erode our trust. The evil one loves to put our focus on what is lacking in our lives to create an attitude of doubt and worry. He does this by asking the same questions He used to tempt Jesus in the wilderness: "Will God be there for You when You are in danger? Will He truly meet Your daily needs? Can God give You the power and influence I can offer? Not sure? Just sell Your soul to me and find out for sure."

How do we counter Satan's attempts? We follow Jesus' example and respond with the true and pure Word of God. One verse that stands out is this one:

> Be strong and courageous. Do not fear or be in dread of them, for it is the LORD your God who goes with you. He will not leave you or forsake you. (Deuteronomy 31:6)

God, in His Word, can replace our worries and fear with courageous confidence in Him. The psalmist reminds us of God's protection: "He only is my rock and my salvation, my fortress; I shall not be shaken. On God rests my salvation and my glory; my mighty rock, my refuge is God. Trust in Him at all times, O people; pour out your heart before Him; God is a refuge for us" (Psalm 62:6–8).

So, what does it mean to be courageous? Joshua, who followed the well-respected leader Moses, needed courage in a time of transition.

The former generation had died off, only a remnant remained: Caleb, Joshua, and Moses. As the transition is underway, Moses was about to go with God. At the end of Deuteronomy 31, Moses gives his farewell words to the people he has loved and led for forty years. Despite all the personal attacks by the chosen and rescued people of God, Moses remained loyal to them. Now Joshua will lead these grumbling and rebellious people as they take the land promised to them. And Moses' dying words to the children of Israel are to have courage because God goes with them.

Is it possible that at the heart of your worry, God is calling you to be courageous? Courageous as you live out your faith in a new school or job, with new peers and a new culture. Your faith may not be well received. You could be mocked, made fun of, even pressured into abandoning your beliefs. Maybe this is your year to lead a courageous life for God and His kingdom. Remember the words Moses gave to Joshua, "Be strong and courageous. . . . It is the LORD who goes before you. He will be with you; He will not leave you or forsake you. Do not fear or be dismayed" (Deuteronomy 31:7–8).

Dear Lord, give me a spirit of courage. I know that whatever You have called me to do, say, or lead, I do it with Your power behind me. Remind me that in my current situation, and in every situation in my future, I can call on You to protect me and to guide me in Your Word. Give me courage, Lord, to live out my calling to expand Your kingdom. And turn my worry into confidence that You are with me every step of the way. In Jesus' name. Amen.

ABOUT YOUR PARENTS

Children, obey your parents in the Lord, for
this is right. Honor your father and mother
(this is the first commandment with a promise),
that it may go well with you and that you
may live long in the land. (EPHESIANS 6:1–3)

When I was growing up, my dad seemed like Superman to me. He was this mythical figure who seemed scary yet heroic. He was always on my side. Even when I was wrong, he would defend me to others and correct me privately. He taught me how to run, think, play baseball, and tell a joke. He was and is my hero.

He wasn't perfect. He may even be called abusive today. He was from a different time when lines were blurred when it came to discipline. He was also an alcoholic, but he gave up drinking because his namesake, me, believed he would.

Our parents are not perfect. They are flawed. They make mistakes. They don't always understand our world or culture. They divorce. They abandon us. They are abusive. They let us down. They sin. They might be good parents. They might be absolute disasters as parents. They might believe that Jesus died for them and be in church every Sunday. Or they might be a bad witness and drop you off for Sunday School on their way to coffee.

You didn't choose your parents. God could have given you any parents, and He gave you the ones you have. Think about that! God gave you your mom and dad. That means He gave them to you specifically for your good, as a gift, to guide you in this life.

You can know that God gave you your parents, and you can trust that they are there for your good because the God who gave you your mom and dad is the same God who gave up His Son to save you. The cross is where your salvation was earned. Good Friday was where your mom and dad's salvation was also achieved. Jesus' Easter is your Easter. Jesus' Easter is your parents' Resurrection Day too.

Your parents are going to sin. They are going to hurt you and let you down. Don't get caught up in their failures—even when they fail you. Try to overlook their flaws. Even better, forgive your parents! That's what God does for you in Jesus. He doesn't treat you as your sins deserve. He doesn't harbor anger forever. He puts all your sins—and your parents' sins—on Jesus. All of them.

In Jesus, you'll also learn to see things differently. Your parents don't want to ruin your life. They don't plan to wreck your popularity with their strange rules and strict curfews. Your parents love you and want you to succeed and turn out to be a good, productive adult. That's why I thanked my dad when I graduated from seminary for how hard he was on me. He made me the person I am. Your parents may be trying to do that for you too!

But if it's impossible to believe in the good intentions of your parents because they've hurt you too much, stop looking at what they've done and look to Jesus instead. He will turn what your parents have done into something good in your life. That's what He promised to do; He works all things together for good for those who love Him (Romans 8:28).

So honor your parents because God commanded you to honor them. Listen to them because God gave them to you. When they speak, remember that God is trying to teach you through them. Your parents are there to give you God's will. If they tell you that a friend isn't healthy for you, try to listen to them. If they suggest a way for you, listen to them unless what they suggest is against God's Word. It usually won't be. After all, they want what's best for you. And they're likely believers just as you are.

One day, then, you are an adult. And you will visit your parents. You will see that they weren't superheroes. They were sinners like you, trying their best for their kids. Have mercy on them. Forgive them. After all, that's the final word Jesus has for you: you're forgiven.

YOUR BODY

> *Or do you not know that your body is a*
> *temple of the Holy Spirit within you, whom*
> *you have from God? You are not your own,*
> *for you were bought with a price. So glorify*
> *God in your body.* (1 CORINTHIANS 6:19–20)

Can I be honest with you for a minute? I don't tell many people this, but I will tell you.

I hate my nose.

It's big for my face, and it's especially disproportionate to my small chin. You know when you see yourself from a different angle for the first time, and it doesn't even look like you? I feel like that every time I see a side-profile picture of myself.

I used to spend a lot of time obsessing over my nose—reading into every comment someone made, analyzing every photograph, inspecting every pore.

But do you know what strangely helps me *not* hate my nose so much? Remembering that it has a purpose—to help me smell!

My nose might be big, but it can definitely smell the cookies I'm baking right now. And spruce trees at Christmastime. And my dog after she's been out in the rain (though I wish I couldn't smell *that* one).

We all have things we wish we could change about our bodies. But thanks to our bodies, we can breathe and smile and laugh and cry and think and feel.

Your stomach that isn't flat still houses your core muscles that help you sit up straight. Your skin might be dotted with acne, but your face can still stretch into a smile. Your arms can still hug people, even if you can't do a push-up. Your legs can still carry you from place to place, even if you have cellulite in your thighs.

Even if you can't think of any positive side to your insecurity, you can always come back to this: you have a body. You may not always love your body, but you always have one. Your body is working hard to keep you alive by pumping blood and inhaling air and firing neurons.

As Christians, we believe the body and the soul are *both* integral to being a person created in the image of God. We are not a body without a soul, nor are we just a soul inhabiting a body. When Jesus came to earth, He inhabited a human body. In order to be true God and true man, He had to have a physical body. Having a body is part of the human experience.

When God created Adam and Eve, He created them in the image of God (Genesis 1:27) and gave them a human form from the dust.

You, too, are created in the image of God. I know that's sometimes hard to believe. Paul writes in 1 Corinthians that our bodies are temples of the Holy Spirit. Our insecurities can't impact how God has created us and what He has created us for! So even when you feel self-conscious or unhappy about your body, maybe you can find a little comfort in knowing that the God who created the mountains and the oceans also created *you*.

A LAMP-LIT PATH

*Your word is a lamp to my feet and
a light to my path.* (PSALM 119:105)

Have you ever walked along a path in the dark? If so, you most likely pulled out your phone and used the flashlight feature to illuminate the path. If you hold the flashlight way up high, you can see far ahead of you. Holding the flashlight above your head shows a large portion of the path.

On the other hand, if you hold the flashlight low, you see just a few feet or even inches ahead of you. Dropping the flashlight down to your feet will show just a part of the path. How high the flashlight is held determines how far ahead you can see.

In our verse above, the psalmist describes God's Word as "a lamp to my feet and a light to my path." God's Word illuminates our path in life. His promises provide a firm foundation for our feet. His presence reminds us that we never walk alone. God's Law keeps us from wandering off the path and into the bramble of sin. God's Gospel proclaims mercy and forgiveness for all the times we have strayed from His path of righteousness. Like a flashlight shining in the darkness, God's Word illuminates our path and gives us confidence for our journey through life.

Nevertheless, God does not promise how much of the path He will illuminate. Yes, God's Word is a light for our path. Yet sometimes, the light shines on only a few feet of it. God never promised to illuminate the whole path so we can see far ahead into the future. Often, God shows only enough of the path to help us take the next step.

Perhaps you are reading this and God has illuminated your path for the next several years. Maybe you have a clear path forward through the next several years through college or work. Thanks be to God that He has revealed a large portion of the path to you!

Perhaps you are reading this and God has illuminated your path for only the next several months. Maybe you know where God is directing your life in the near future, but not in the distant future. Press on and know that God will further illuminate your steps when you get there!

Perhaps you are reading this and God has illuminated your path for only the next couple of days or hours. This can be a hard place to be. Maybe you do not know where God is leading your life tomorrow. (Truth be told, we are all in this place; we don't really know what God has planned for us tomorrow.) Take heart and know that He is still leading you through His promises and mercy.

No matter what, God's Word guides our path. Even if you cannot see the whole path ahead, know that you never walk alone: "He will not leave you or forsake you" (Deuteronomy 31:6). It's much easier making a hard decision, going to college, or beginning a new job knowing that Jesus is with you. He knows where He is going. He knows where He is leading you. Journey on!

Finally, be strong in the Lord and

in the strength of His might.

(EPHESIANS 6:10)